The Bill of Rights

CORE DOCUMENTS

The Bill of Rights

~ CORE DOCUMENTS ~

Selected and Introduced by

Gordon Lloyd

ASHBROOK PRESS

Copyright © 2018 Ashbrook Center, Ashland University

Library of Congress Cataloging-in-Publication Data
The Bill of Rights: Core Documents; Selected and Introduced by Gordon Lloyd
   p.   cm.
Includes Index
1. United States—Politics and government.
ISBN 978-1-878802-41-5 (pbk.)

Cover images, above the title, left to right:
Portrait of George Mason, by Dominic Boudet, 1811, after a lost portrait
  by John Hesselius, ca. 1750. Courtesy of Gunston Hall.
Roger Sherman, by Ralph Earl, circa 1775. Yale University Art Gallery. LCCN: n79129213
James Madison, Jr., by Bradley Stevens, after Charles Wilson Peale, 2002.
  Collection of the US House of Representatives. 2002.048.000.
Associate Justice James Wilson, by Robert S. Susan, after Leopold
  G. Seyffert, after Max Rosenthal, circa 1936. Courtesy of the
  Collection of the Supreme Court of the United States.
Alexander Hamilton, by John Trumbull, 1900–1912. Library
  of Congress, LC-DIG-det-4a26167.

Cover image, below the title:
The Bill of Rights, photograph of original manuscript, ca. 1920–1930.
  Library of Congress Prints and Photographs Division, LC-USP6-
  360A, http://www.loc.gov/pictures/resource/cph.3a04470/.

Interior design/composition: Brad Walrod/Kenoza Type, Inc.

Ashbrook Center at Ashland University
401 College Avenue
Ashland, Ohio 44805
www.ashbrook.or

ABOUT THE ASHBROOK CENTER

The Ashbrook Center restores and strengthens the capacities of the American people for constitutional self-government. Ashbrook teaches students and teachers across our country what America is and what she represents in the long history of the world. Offering a variety of resources and programs, Ashbrook is the largest university-based educator in the enduring principles and practice of free government. Dedicated in 1983 by President Ronald Reagan, the Ashbrook Center is governed by its own board and responsible for raising all of the funds necessary for its many programs.

Visit us online at Ashbrook.org, TeachingAmericanHistory.org, ReligionInAmerica.org, and 50coredocs.org.

Contents

General Editor's Introduction

This collection of documents on the Bill of Rights is part of the Ashbrook Center's extended series of document collections covering major periods, themes, and institutions in American history and government. It is the third of four volumes that will cover the Founding of the United States. *The American Founding*, already published, is the capstone of the four. The others—the volume on the Constitutional Convention, also already published; this collection; and a volume on the ratification of the Constitution, which will follow it—tell aspects of the founding story in more detail. The documents in this collection provide historical background on the rights the colonists claimed to hold, and why and how those rights became the rights enshrined in the first ten amendments to the Constitution. It focuses on the argument over whether a bill of rights was necessary, as this argument revealed much about the founding generation's view of government and, in particular, the federal arrangement in the Constitution. Together, the four volumes on the Founding provide the essentials for understanding the Founding as the Founders understood it.

When the series of Ashbrook document collections is complete, it will be comprehensive and authoritative because it will present America's story in the words of those who wrote it—America's presidents, labor leaders, farmers, philosophers, industrialists, politicians, workers, explorers, religious leaders, judges, soldiers; its slaveholders and abolitionists; its expansionists and isolationists; its reformers and stand-patters; its strict and broad constructionists; its hard-eyed realists and visionary utopians—all united in their commitment to equality and liberty, yet all also divided often by their different understandings of these most fundamental American ideas. The documents are about all this—the still unfinished American experiment with self-government.

As this volume does, each of the volumes in the series will contain key documents on its period, theme, or institution, selected by an expert and reviewed by an editorial board. Each volume will have an introduction highlighting key documents and themes. In an appendix to each volume, there will also be a thematic table of contents, showing the connections between various documents. Another appendix will provide study questions for each document, as well questions that refer to other documents in the collection, tying them together as the thematic table of contents does. Each document will be checked against an authoritative original source and have an introduction outlining its significance. We will provide notes to each document to identify people, events, movements, or ideas that may be unfamiliar to non-specialist readers and to improve understanding of the document's historical context. As with *The American Founding*, this volume contains as appendices the Declaration of Independence and the Constitution, as well as suggestions for further reading.

Gordon Lloyd, Senior Fellow at the Ashbrook Center, selected the documents and wrote the introductions, notes, and study questions. David Tucker was the general editor. Joan Livingston was the copyeditor. Lisa Ormiston of the Ashbrook Center oversaw production. This publication was made possible through the support of a grant by the John Templeton Foundation. The opinions expressed in this publication are those of the editors and do not necessarily reflect the views of the John Templeton Foundation.

David Tucker, Senior Fellow
Ashbrook Center

Introduction

There is a strong temptation to consider the story of the U.S. Bill of Rights as part of a larger narrative that starts with Magna Carta in 1215 and continues into the twenty-first century with concerns about human rights across the globe, touching briefly on how Americans introduced and passed a bill of rights. The chronological focus of these twenty-six selections is narrower: the context is primarily between 1776 and 1791.

Thus the larger question of how the British and colonial heritage fits into the American story is covered only briefly (Documents 1–2). Of considerable importance in this brief account is that the rights included in the Massachusetts Body of Liberties (1641) are, numerically, more significant than those found in Magna Carta (1215) and the English Bill of Rights (1689). And so too are the rights enumerated in the Maryland Toleration Acts. We include these two colonial documents to remind the reader that Americans were concerned about rights, especially religious rights, even before the founding era of 1776–1791. Three rights are unanimously represented in all the state constitutions: the right of conscience/free exercise of religion; the right to have one's case heard by a local impartial jury; and the due process rights of the common law. The framers of the new state documents decided these last rights were no longer secure under the traditional governmental arrangements. We consider it significant that the new states declared themselves to be republican and that the purpose of a republican government was to secure rights.

Seven states attached a prefatory declaration of rights to the frame of government: Virginia (June 1776), Delaware (September 1776), Pennsylvania (September 1776), Maryland (November 1776), North Carolina (December 1776), Massachusetts (March 1780), and New Hampshire (June 1784). These declarations were, in effect, a preamble stating the purposes for which the people had chosen the particular form of government. There was a remarkable uniformity among the seven states with regard to the kinds of civil and criminal rights they sought to secure.

Four states decided not to preface their republican constitutions with a declaration of rights: New Jersey (July 1776), Georgia (February 1777), New York (April 1777), and South Carolina (March 1778). Nevertheless, each incorporated individual protections in their constitutions.

Virginia entered unfamiliar territory with the disestablishment of the
Anglican Church in 1779. Nevertheless, there were two competing models to which legislators could turn. The Massachusetts model endorsed the
establishment of the Christian Protestant religion and, to that end, the legislature was constitutionally mandated to tax inhabitants for the support of
public religious instruction. The taxpayer, nevertheless, was free to name
the specific religion that was to receive the assessment. On the other hand,
the Pennsylvania model warned that such taxation threatened the right of
an individual to the free exercise of religion. In December 1784, the Virginia
Assembly considered an assessment bill, consistent with the Massachusetts
model, that would financially support the propagation of Christianity as the
state religion. James Madison objected. The author of a protest addressed to
the Virginia Assembly (Document 7), Madison urged the legislators to reject
the proposed legislation. In the process, Madison pushed the national conversation even further in the direction of individual free exercise of religion
and away from community-endorsed religion. The practical manifestation of
Madison's efforts was the Virginia Assembly's adoption in 1785 of Jefferson's
Statute of Religious Liberty introduced in 1779. The Virginia Senate passed
the statute in January 1786. It is also important to note how these rights made
their way into the Northwest Ordinance (Document 8).

A year after the passage of the Virginia statute at the Constitutional Convention (May to September 1787), the first of George Mason's ten objections
to the Constitution began: "There is no declaration of rights" (Document 9).
In particular, "there is no declaration of any kind for preserving liberty of
the press, the trial by jury in civil cases, nor against the danger of standing
armies in times of peace." Mason's position was that a federal bill of rights
was both imperative and valuable. He was concerned that Congress might
abuse the supremacy and the necessary and proper clauses of the Constitution (Articles 6 and 1, section 8, respectively). The supremacy clause made
federal laws "paramount to the laws and constitutions of the several states."
Thus, "the declaration of rights, in the separate states, are of no security."
The necessary and proper clause enabled Congress to "grant monopolies
in trade and commerce, constitute new crimes, inflict unusual and severe
punishments, and extend their power as far as they should think proper."

Throughout the nine-month ratification campaign, proponents of the
Constitution defended the absence of a bill of rights. James Wilson's State
House Speech (Document 10), delivered in Philadelphia three weeks after the
Constitutional Convention adjourned, articulated what came to be known
as the Federalist position: a bill of rights is unnecessary and dangerous.

Wilson argued that at the state level, a bill of rights was necessary and salutary because "everything which is not reserved, is given," but "superfluous and absurd" at the federal level because "everything which is not given, is reserved." Wilson's speech became the foil for the Antifederalist opposition literature in the fall of 1787 (Documents 11–15). Near the end of the ratification campaign, Federalist 84 (Document 19) repeated Wilson's insistence that a republican form of government had no need for a bill of rights because such bills "are, in their origin, stipulations between kings and their subjects, abridgments of prerogative in favor of privilege, reservations of rights not surrendered to the prince."

By early January 1788, the ratifying conventions in Delaware (voting 30–0), Pennsylvania (46–23), New Jersey (38–0), Georgia (26–0), and Connecticut (128–40) had ratified the Constitution. The report issued by the twenty-three Pennsylvania opponents had a considerable impact on the subsequent campaign (Document 15). The report proposed two different kinds of amendments. On the one hand, the minority called for amendments that would re-establish the principles of the Articles of Confederation. These were unfriendly to the Constitution. On the other hand, they proposed that a declaration of rights be annexed to the Constitution. These were friendly amendments. What became drafts of the first, fourth, fifth, sixth, seventh, and eighth amendments to the Constitution were included in their list, although the origin of these amendments can be traced to colonial documents and state constitutions.

The fate of the Constitution was determined in the Massachusetts, New Hampshire, Virginia, and New York ratifying conventions in the first half of 1788. Antifederalist literature in the fall of 1787 had had an adverse effect on the campaign for ratification. A compromise—"ratify now, amend later"—was needed in each of these four states to secure ratification (Documents 17–18). In Massachusetts, ten delegates switched their votes and a 187–168 majority ratified the Constitution. A switch of five votes ensured ratification in both New Hampshire (57–47) and Virginia (89–79). In New York, the Antifederalists outnumbered the Federalists by a margin of 46–19 going into the convention; but in the end, the Constitution was ratified by a vote of 30–27.

The Antifederalist opposition and friends of the Constitution made two different kinds of recommendations. First, some called for an alteration in the very structure and powers of the new federal government. Second, others sought to protect the rights of individuals with respect to the federal government. All nine of Massachusetts's recommendations are of the first kind. New Hampshire was the first to add a brief declaration of the rights of

citizens to the list of amendments. In Virginia and New York, the two kinds
of amendments were explicitly separated.

With the ratification of the Constitution, James Madison (1751–1836), who
had done so much to bring it into existence,[1] supported the adoption of a
bill of rights, while objecting to amendments that would radically alter the
new government's structure and power (Document 22). He did so for both
theoretical and prudential reasons. Madison distanced himself from Wilson's
argument that a bill of rights might be dangerous as well as unnecessary. He
overcame the danger of listing rights—the list might be seen as definitive
and thus limit the rights of citizens rather than protect them—by declaring
that the enumeration "of certain rights, shall not be construed to deny or
disparage others retained by the people." This eventually became the Ninth
Amendment and is a wholly Madison contribution. The prudential reasons
included conciliating "honorable and patriotic" opponents who wanted to
"revise" the Constitution by including a bill of rights and defeating the call for
a second convention that would "abolish" the Constitution (Document 21).
He saw the First Congress as the "proper mode" to accomplish the objective

---

[1] Madison, known as "the Father of the Constitution," is at the heart of our documentary account of the origin and politics of the Bill of Rights, from Virginia in
1776 to the First Congress in 1789. During this time, Madison's position on the Bill
of Rights changed, at least in part because of his relationship with Jefferson. To see
the importance of this relationship, we must place it in the context of Virginia politics, which provide the bookends to the story of the Bill of Rights. George Mason
wrote the Virginia Declaration of Rights in June 1776 (with Madison's suggested
alteration to the right of conscience clause). The Declaration of Rights was one
influence on Jefferson as he wrote the Declaration of Independence. Mason also
proposed to the Constitutional Convention that a bill of rights be adopted. Madison opposed Mason in the Convention on the issue. A few years later, in December
1791, Virginia finally adopted the Bill of Rights, with Madison as the leader of those
favoring adoption and Mason in opposition. Why did Virginia start the process, take
the lead in the debates, and then delay so long to ratify the Bill of Rights? The answer
is an irreconcilable divide among Antifederalists. There were those who wanted to
change fundamentally the new American system and those who were friendly to
the Constitution. The latter wanted to restrain the new government with a bill of
rights. Between 1787 and 1791, Mason became one of those who wanted fundamental
change, while Madison, always a friend to the Constitution, became one of those
willing to amend it by adding a bill of rights. He made this change with the help of
Jefferson (Documents 16, 20–22). See the companion volumes *The American Founding: Core Documents* (Ashland, Ohio: Ashbrook Press, 2017) and *The Constitutional
Convention: Core Documents* (Ashland, Ohio: Ashbrook Press, 2018), both edited
by Gordon Lloyd.

of revision. What joined together the theoretical and prudential reasons was that Madison did not want a second convention to take place.

The correspondence between Madison in the United States and Thomas Jefferson in Paris is a critical part of the story of the adoption of the Bill of Rights, from the signing of the Constitution through the ratification campaign and into the First Congress (Documents 16, 20, and 21). In his October 24, 1788 letter, Madison summarized the political and ethical problem that was to be solved by the Constitution: "To prevent instability and injustice in the legislation of the states." What Madison was able to achieve, he explained to Jefferson, was the creation of an extended republic that would secure the civil and religious rights of individuals from the danger of majority faction. Jefferson responded favorably toward the proposed Constitution two months later. He was troubled, however, by Wilson's argument that a bill of rights was unnecessary. He reminded Madison that "a bill of rights is what the people are entitled to against every government on earth, general or particular; and what no just government should refuse, or rest on inference." He listed six essential rights that should be declared: "freedom of religion, freedom of the press, protection against standing armies, restriction of monopolies, the eternal and unremitting force of the habeas corpus laws, and trials by jury in all matters." Jefferson reiterated the importance of including his list of six rights upon being informed by Madison that the Constitution had been adopted.

In his first Inaugural Address (April 30, 1789), George Washington addressed only two particular issues: his compensation, which he declined, and Congress' "exercise of the occasional power delegated by the fifth article of the Constitution," the power to amend the Constitution. He asked that "whilst you carefully avoid every alteration which might endanger the benefits of an united and effective government, a reverence for the characteristic rights of freemen will sufficiently influence your deliberations on the question, how far the former can be impregnably fortified or the latter be safely and advantageously promoted." Madison followed Washington's recommendation of proposing a bill of rights that, at the same time, did not alter the work of the Constitutional Convention. That became Madison's challenge in the First Congress (Document 22).

The House of Representatives debate on Madison's propositions is not without irony (Document 23). Roger Sherman, arguably Madison's leading and most persuasive opponent during the structural phase of the 1787 Philadelphia Convention, objected to Madison's attempt to incorporate the bill of right additions "neatly" within the body of the Constitution. If the revisions are added as "supplements," or amendments to the Constitution, argued Madison, "they will create unfavorable comparison" with the original Constitution. Sherman, however, prevailed. The original work of the framers, he argued, should remain intact. Moreover, Sherman urged his colleagues to reject incorporating the Declaration of Independence into the Preamble: "The words 'We the people,' in the original Constitution, are as copious and expressive as possible; any addition will only drag out the sentence without illuminating it." On the other hand, Sherman proved to be an important ally in defeating the attempts of the South Carolina delegation to intro-duce amendments that would "change the principles of the government." The Senate reduced the number of amendment proposals from seventeen to twelve. In doing so, the Senate defeated Madison's House-backed pro-posal to protect freedom of conscience and the press at the state and national levels, restricting the protection to the national level only. The Senate also combined the protection of conscience and the press into one amendment (Document 24). The Senate version was adopted, with slight revision, by the whole Congress and submitted as twelve amendments to the states for approval (Document 25). Ten were ratified by three-fourths of the state leg-islatures (Document 26).

Very important from Madison's perspective, Richard Henry Lee and Wil-liam Grayson—both radical Antifederalists and the only Antifederalists in the United States Senate—were totally unsuccessful in their effort to move the power and structure of the Constitution back in the direction of the Articles of Confederation. They preferred this to adopting a bill of rights that would reinforce the idea that the Constitution was a limiting as well as an empowering document.

For his part, Madison was less than completely successful with his bill of rights proposals. Few members shared Madison's urgent feeling that friendly alterations must be sent to the states by the end of the first session. The rights did not end up located in the Constitution where he wanted them to be. The number of rights was reduced from Madison's original list (Document 22) and several clauses, the religion clauses in particular, underwent close scru-tiny and major alteration. Madison's attempt to have the states as well as the nation restrained in the area of conscience, press, and jury was defeated in the Senate. The Bill of Rights, as adopted, applied only to the federal gov-ernment. So the appellation "Father of the Bill of Rights" ought to be cau-tiously used. Yet it is certainly true that Madison's persistence was critical to twelve amendments being sent to the states for adoption by the end of the first session and, not coincidentally, for the subsequent adoption of the original Constitution by North Carolina and Rhode Island.

The adoption of the Bill of Rights was a mixture principle and politics.[2] It did not just fall from the sky in one whole and intelligible form. True, the Bill of Rights incorporated much of the English common law and the colonial due process tradition, but it also shed much of this tradition's feudal and monarchical features. Also, Americans between 1776 and 1791 appealed beyond their traditions to support freedom of conscience, free speech, and enhanced rights of due process of law.

---

[2] James Madison to Richard Peters, August 19, 1789, https://goo.gl/Kosg4H. This letter, organized around seven themes, is a model of principled leadership at its best; it joins that which is necessary with that which is proper.

The Bill of Rights

CORE DOCUMENTS

The Massachusetts Body of Liberties

December 1641

T he Massachusetts Body of Liberties, adopted in December 1641, was the first attempt in the colonies to restrain the power of the elected representatives by appealing to a fundamental document that lists the rights and duties of the people. The document, drafted and debated over several years, combined the early American covenanting tradition of the Mayflower Compact with an appeal to the common law tradition that crossed the Atlantic from Britain. The Massachusetts Body of Liberties contains ninety-eight sections. It covers the rules concerning judicial proceedings (sections 18–57); "liberties more peculiarly concerning the free man" (sections 58–78); and the rights of women (79–80), children (81–84), servants (85–88), foreigners (89–91), and animals (92–93). Section 94 provides biblical justification supporting the death penalty in twelve cases, and Section 95 contains eleven liberties given by "the Lord Jesus...to the Churches." The most enduring part of the Body of Liberties is the preamble and the first seventeen sections, reproduced here.

SOURCE: The complete version can be found in W. H. Whitemore, *The Colonial Laws of Massachusetts*, 1889 (33–46). See also *The Essential Bill of Rights*, edited by Gordon Lloyd and Margie Lloyd, (Lanham, MD: University Press of America, 1998), 38–40. The numbered paragraphs are in the original.

The free fruition of such liberties, immunities and privileges as humanity, civility, and Christianity call for as due to every man in his place and proportion without impeachment and infringement hath ever been and ever will be the tranquility and stability of churches and commonwealths. And the denial or deprival thereof, the disturbance if not the ruin of both.

We hold it therefore our duty and safety whilst we are about the further establishing of this government to collect and express all such freedoms as for present we foresee may concern us, and our posterity after us, and to ratify them with our solemn consent.

We do therefore this day religiously and unanimously decree and confirm these following rights, liberties and privileges concerning our churches, and civil state to be respectively impartially and inviolably enjoyed and observed throughout our jurisdiction forever.

1. No man's life shall be taken away, no man's honor or good name shall be stained, no man's person shall be arrested, restrained, banished, dismembered, nor any ways punished, no man shall be deprived of his wife or children, no man's goods or estate shall be taken away from him, nor any way indammaged under color of law or countenance of authority, unless it be by virtue or equity of some express law of the country warranting the same, established by a general court and sufficiently published, or in case of the defect of a law in any particular case by the word of God. And in capital cases, or in cases concerning dismembering or banishment according to that word to be judged by the general court.

2. Every person within this jurisdiction, whether inhabitant or foreigner shall enjoy the same justice and law, that is general for the plantation, which we constitute and execute one towards another without partiality or delay.

3. No man shall be urged to take any oath or subscribe any articles, covenants or remonstrance, of a public and civil nature, but such as the general court hath considered, allowed, and required.

4. No man shall be punished for not appearing at or before any civil assembly, court, council, magistrate, or officer, nor for the omission of any office or service, if he shall be necessarily hindered by any apparent act or providence of God, which he could neither foresee nor avoid. Provided that this law shall not prejudice any person of his just cost or damage, in any civil action.

5. No man shall be compelled to any public work or service unless the press be grounded upon some act of the general court, and have reasonable allowance therefore.

6. No man shall be pressed in person to any office, work, wars or other public service, that is necessarily and sufficiently exempted by any natural or personal impediment, as by want of years, greatness of age, defect of mind, failing of senses, or impotency of limbs.

7. No man shall be compelled to go out of the limits of this plantation upon any offensive wars which this commonwealth or any of our friends or confederates shall voluntarily undertake. But only

upon such vindictive and defensive wars in our own behalf or the behalf of our friends and confederates as shall be enterprised by the counsel and consent of a court general, or by authority derived from the same.

8. No man's cattle or goods of what kind soever shall be pressed or taken for any public use or service, unless it be by warrant grounded upon some act of the general court, nor without such reasonable prices and hire as the ordinary rates of the country do afford. And if his cattle or goods shall perish or suffer damage in such service, the owner shall be sufficiently recompensed.

9. No monopolies shall be granted or allowed amongst us, but of such new Inventions that are profitable to the country, and that for a short time.

10. All our lands and heritages shall be free from all fines and licenses upon alienations, and from all hariotts, wardships, liveries, primer-seisins, year day and wast, escheates, and forfeitures,[1] upon the deaths of parents or ancestors, be they natural, casual or Judicial.

11. All persons which are of the age of 21 years, and of right understanding and memories, whether excommunicate or condemned[2] shall have full power and liberty to make their wills and testaments, and other lawful alienations of their lands and estates.

12. Every man whether inhabitant or foreigner, free or not free shall have liberty to come to any public court, counsel or town meeting, and either by speech or writing to move any lawful, seasonable, and material question, or to present any necessary motion, complaint, petition, bill or information, whereof that meeting hath proper cognizance, so it be done in convenient time, due order, and respective manner.

13. No man shall be rated[3] here for any estate or revenue he hath in England, or in any foreign parts till it be transported hither.

---

[1] All of these English law terms refer to different ways, under different circumstances, that an individual or his heirs could be forced to surrender property or pay fees to the king. They are of feudal origin.

[2] Deprived of membership in the church, which could mean deprived of certain civil rights or protections, or condemned to death

[3] taxed

14. Any conveyance or alienation of land or other estate whatsoever, made by any woman that is married, any child under age, idiot or distracted person, shall be good if it be passed and ratified by the consent of a general court.

15. All covenous[4] or fraudulent alienations or conveyances of lands, tenements, or any heriditaments,[5] shall be of no validity to defeat any man from due debts or legacies, or from any just title, claim or possession, of that which is so fraudulently conveyed.

16. Every inhabitant that is a householder shall have free fishing and fowling in any great ponds and bays, coves and rivers, so far as the sea ebbs and flows within the precincts of the town where they dwell, unless the free men of the same town or the General Court have otherwise appropriated them, provided that this shall not be extended to give leave to any man to come upon others' propriety without their leave.

17. Every man of or within this jurisdiction shall have free liberty, notwithstanding any civil power remove both himself, and his family at their pleasure out of the same, provided there be no legal impediment to the contrary.

---

[4] deceptive or fraudulent
[5] any property

DOCUMENT 2

The Maryland Act Concerning Religion

April 21, 1649

The act was passed by the Maryland Assembly on April 21, 1649, and confirmed by the Lord Proprietary on August 26, 1650. The first four paragraphs emphasize the centrality of the Christian religion to a well-governed commonwealth. The last two paragraphs provide protection for the "free exercise" of religion—that is, free exercise for any Christian.

The 1649 Maryland Act Concerning Religion—also known popularly as the Toleration Act—is a good example of the paradoxical relationship in America between the establishment of religion and the free exercise of religion. This paradox—both the public establishment of religion and the individual right of conscience were supported simultaneously at various times among the colonies—emerged during the colonial experience. It became controversial only in the 1780s, when pressure grew for disestablishment (Document 7).

The first two thirds of the act established the importance of the public recognition of the Christian religion for "a well-governed" commonwealth. In fact, the freemen and the governor expressly state the "serious" causal connection between the promotion of political virtue and respect for established religion. To that end, provision is made for the punishment of a series of violations ranging from death in the case of blaspheming God to a fine for profaning the Sabbath. The 1649 act established the public centrality of Christianity without designating preferential treatment for one Christian sect. When Lord Baltimore's property became a royal colony in 1702, the establishment portion of the paradox acquired an additional dimension. The Church of England became the established sect in 1702.

The last third of the act recognizes the theological and political importance of religious toleration, including severe penalties to be levied against individuals who violate the free exercise of religion clause. These include reparations to be paid by the wrongdoer to the person whose individual right to freedom of conscience has been violated. The Maryland Act not only explicitly uses the phrase "free exercise" of religion but does so at least one hundred years before the enlightenment argument that the free exercise of religion was a natural right.

SOURCE: *Proceedings and Acts of the General Assembly of Maryland, 1637–1664* (Baltimore: Maryland Historical Society, 1883) vol. I: 244–247.

Forasmuch as in a well-governed and Xpian [Christian] commonwealth matters concerning religion and the honor of God ought in the first place to be taken, into serious consideration and endeavored to be settled. Be it therefore ordered and enacted by the Right Hoble [Honorable] Cecilius Lord Baron of Baltimore absolute lord and proprietary of this province with the advise and consent of this General Assembly. That whatsoever person or persons within this province and the islands thereunto belonging shall from henceforth blaspheme God, that is curse him, or deny our Savior Jesus Christ to be the son of God, or shall deny the Holy Trinity the father, Son, and Holy Ghost, or the God-head of any of the said three persons of the Trinity or the unity of the Godhead, or shall use or utter any reproachful speeches, words or language concerning the said Holy Trinity, or any of the said three persons thereof, shall be punished with death and confiscation or forfeiture of all his or her lands and goods to the Lord Proprietary and his heirs.

And be it also enacted by the authority and with the advice and assent aforesaid, that whatsoever person or persons shall from henceforth use or utter any reproachful words or speeches concerning the blessed Virgin Mary the Mother of our Savior or the holy Apostles or Evangelists or any of them shall in such case for the first offense forfeit to the said Lord Proprietary and his heirs lords and proprietaries of this province the sum of five pound sterling or the value thereof to be levied on the goods and chattels of every such person so offending, but in case such offender or offenders, shall not then have goods and chattels sufficient for the satisfying of such forfeiture, or that the same be not otherwise speedily satisfied[,] that then such offender or offenders shall be publicly whipped and bee imprisoned during the pleasure of the Lord Proprietary or the Lieutenant or chief Governor of this province for the time being. And that every such offender or offenders for every second offence shall forfeit ten pound sterling or the value thereof to be levied as aforesaid, or in case such offender or offenders shall not then have goods and chattels within this province sufficient for that purpose then to be publicly and severely whipped and imprisoned as before is expressed. And that every person or persons before mentioned offending herein the third time, shall for such third offense forfeit all his lands and goods and be for ever banished and expelled out of this province.

And be it also further enacted by the same authority advice and assent that whatsoever person or persons shall from henceforth upon any occasion of offense or otherwise in a reproachful manner or way declare, call or denominate any person or persons whatsoever inhabiting residing trafficking trading or commercing within this province[,] or within any ports, harbors, creeks or havens to the same belonging[,] an heretic, schismatic, idolater, Puritan, Independent, Presbyterian, Popish priest, Jesuit, Jesuited Papist, Lutheran, Calvinist, Anabaptist, Brownist, Antinomian, Barrowist, Roundhead, Separatist[1] or any other name or term in a reproachful manner relating to matter of religion shall for every such offense forfeit and lose the sum of ten shillings sterling or the value thereof to be levied on the goods and chattels of every such offender and offenders, the one half thereof to be forfeited and paid unto the person and persons of whom such reproachful words are or shall be spoken or uttered, and the other half thereof to the Lord Proprietary and his heirs lords and proprietaries of this province. But if such person or persons who shall at any time utter or speak any such reproachful words or language shall not have goods or chattels sufficient and overt within this province to be taken to satisfy the penalty aforesaid or that the same bee not otherwise speedily satisfied, that then the person or persons so offending shall be publicly whipped, and shall suffer imprisonment without bail or maineprise[2] until he, she, or they respectively shall satisfy the party so offended or grieved by such reproachful language by asking him or her respectively forgiveness publicly for such his offense before the magistrate or chief officer or officers of the town or place where such offence shall be given.

And be it further likewise enacted by the authority and consent aforesaid that every person or persons within this province that shall at any time hereafter profane the Sabbath or Lords day called Sunday by frequent swearing, drunkenness or by any uncivil or disorderly recreation, or by working on that day when absolute necessity doth not require it, shall be every such first offense forfeit 2s. 6d sterling or the value thereof, and for the second offence 5s sterling or the value thereof, and for the third offence and so for every time he shall offend in like manner afterwards 10s sterling or the value thereof. And in case such offender and offenders shall not have sufficient goods or chattels within this province to satisfy any of the said penalties respectively hereby imposed for profaning the Sabbath or Lords day called Sunday as aforesaid, that in every such case the party so offending shall for the first and second offense in that kind be imprisoned till he or she shall publicly in

---

[1] Except for "Popish priest, Jesuit, Jesuited Papist," which refer to Roman Catholic priests, these terms all refer to various kinds of Protestants not members of the Anglican church established in Britain. An "Antinomian" is someone who believes that the gift of grace removes the obligation to obey the moral law.

[2] Release of a prisoner to someone taking responsibility for the prisoner once released.

open court before the chief commander judge or magistrate, of that county, town or precinct where such offence shall be committed acknowledge the scandal and offense he hath in that respect given against God and the good and civil government of this province. And for the third offence and for every time after shall also be publicly whipped. And whereas the enforcing of the conscience in matters of religion hath frequently fallen out to be of dangerous consequence in those commonwealths where it hath been practiced, and for the more quiet and peaceable government of this province, and the better to preserve mutual Love and amity amongst the inhabitants thereof[:]

Be it therefore also by the Lord Proprietary with the advice and consent of this assembly ordained & enacted (except as in this present act is before declared and set forth) that no person or persons whatsoever within this province, or the islands, ports, harbors, creeks, or havens thereunto belonging professing to believe in Jesus Christ, shall from henceforth be any ways troubled, molested or discountenanced for or in respect of his or her religion nor in the free exercise thereof within this province or the islands thereunto belonging nor any way compelled to the belief or exercise of any other religion against his or her consent, so as they be not unfaithful to the lord proprietary, or molest or conspire against the civil government established or to be established in this province under him or his heirs. And that all & every person and persons that shall presume contrary to this act and the true intent and meaning thereof directly or indirectly either in person or estate willfully to wrong disturb trouble or molest any person whatsoever within this province professing to believe in Jesus Christ for or in respect of his or her religion or the free exercise thereof within this province other than is provided for in this act that such person or persons so offending, shall be compelled to pay treble damages to the party so wronged or molested, and for every such offence shall also forfeit 20s sterling in money or the value thereof, half thereof for the use of the Lord Proprietary, and his heirs lords and proprietaries of this province, and the other half for the use of the party so wronged or molested as aforesaid. Or if the party so offending as aforesaid shall refuse or be unable to recompense the party so wronged, or to satisfy such fine or forfeiture, then such offender shall be severely punished by public whipping & imprisonment during the pleasure of the Lord Proprietary, or his Lieutenant or chief Governor of this Province for the time being without bail or maineprise.

And be it further also enacted by the authority and consent aforesaid that the sheriff or other officer or officers from time to time to be appointed & authorized for that purpose of the county, town or precinct where every particular offense in this present act contained shall happen at any time to be committed and whereupon there is hereby a forfeiture, fine or penalty imposed shall from time to time distrain and seize the goods and estate of every such person so offending as aforesaid against this present act or any part thereof, and sell the same or any part thereof for the full satisfaction of such forfeiture, fine, or penalty as aforesaid, restoring unto the party so offending the remainder or overplus of the said goods or estate after such satisfaction so made as aforesaid.

The freemen have assented. Thomas Hatton
Enacted by the Governor William Stone

Virginia Declaration of Rights and Constitution

June 12 and 29, 1776

The House of Burgesses adopted the Virginia Declaration of Rights in June 1776. Among the delegates were George Mason, the most important contributor, and twenty-five-year-old James Madison, who drafted the section on the "free exercise of religion." Also present at the creation of the Virginia Declaration and Constitution were John Blair and Edmund Randolph. Eleven years later, these four delegates were chosen to be part of the seven-member Virginia delegation to the Constitutional Convention.

The "rights" listed in the first five sections might strike the contemporary reader as odd; it is important to remember, however, that among the most fundamental rights articulated by the revolutionary generation was the right of the people to choose their form of government. Note the articulation of the separation of powers doctrine. Sections 6 through 14 cover familiar ground. Most of the civil rights and criminal procedures listed were part of the Americanized version of the "rights of Englishmen" tradition. Section 15 reflects the traditional republican argument that free government could survive only if the people were virtuous. Because colonial America turned to religion to perform this important political function, there was a presumption that religion had an "established" status. In 1776, the Anglican Church was the established church of Virginia, and there is nothing in the Virginia Declaration of Rights that challenges this establishment. On the other hand, Madison incorporated into Section 16 an argument for the free exercise of religion, claiming that "the duty which we owe to our CREATOR, and the manner of discharging it, can be directed only by reason and conviction, not by force or violence." This assertion challenges the establishment of any particular sect, even for the purpose of inculcating the morality that Madison elsewhere argued was essential to republican government.

The same convention also framed and adopted the Virginia Constitution. The first, and longest, section anticipates the Declaration of Independence (Appendix C): twenty-one separate indictments are listed against King George. Section 2 provides the authorization for establishing a new foundation. Sections 3–8 and 10–12 pertain to the bicameral legislature; and most of the remaining sections focus on the election, appointment, or removal of executive and judicial officers. Section 21 *lays the foundation for the Northwest Ordinance (Document 8) by ceding western lands disputed between Virginia and other states to the latter and by anticipating the creation of new states in the western territory of which Virginia held title. (The Confederation Congress passed the ordinance, which laid the plan for settling the western territory and admitting sections of it as new states, in 1787.)*

SOURCE: We have followed W. W. Hening, *Statutes at Large* (Richmond, VA: George Cochran, 1823), vol. 9:109–19, and added section numbers to the Virginia Constitution. These sections are identified by Roman numerals. The Arabic numerals identifying the separate sections of the Declaration of Rights are in the original.

A DECLARATION OF RIGHTS made by the representatives of the good people of Virginia, assembled in full and free convention; which rights do pertain to them and their posterity, as the basis and foundation of government.

1. That all men are by nature equally free and independent, and have certain inherent rights, of which, when they enter into a state of society, they cannot, by any compact, deprive or divest their posterity; namely, the enjoyment of life and liberty, with the means of acquiring and possessing property, and pursuing and obtaining happiness and safety.
2. That all power is vested in, and consequently derived from, the people; that magistrates are their trustees and servants, and at all times amenable to them.
3. That government is, or ought to be, instituted for the common benefit, protection, and security of the people, nation, or community; of all the various modes and forms of government, that is best, which is capable of producing the greatest degree of happiness and safety, and is most effectually secured against the danger of maladministration; and that whenever any government shall be found inadequate or contrary to these purposes, a majority of the community hath an indubitable, unalienable, and indefeasible right, to reform, alter, or abolish it, in such manner as shall be judged most conducive to the public weal.[1]
4. That no man, or set of men, are entitled to exclusive or separate emoluments and privileges from the community, but in

---

[1] welfare

consideration of public services; which, not being descendible,[2] neither ought the offices of magistrate, legislator, or judge to be hereditary.

5. That the legislative and executive powers of the state should be separate and distinct from the judiciary; and that the members of the two first may be restrained from oppression, by feeling and participating the burthens[3] of the people, they should, at fixed periods, be reduced to a private station, return into that body from which they were originally taken, and the vacancies be supplied by frequent, certain, and regular elections, in which all, or any part of the former members, to be again eligible, or ineligible, as the laws shall direct.

6. That elections of members to serve as representatives of the people, in assembly, ought to be free; and that all men, having sufficient evidence of permanent common interest with, and attachment to, the community, have the right of suffrage, and cannot be taxed or deprived of their property for public uses without their own consent, or that of their representative so elected, nor bound by any law to which they have not, in like manner, assented, for the public good.

7. That all power of suspending laws, or the execution of laws, by any authority, without consent of the representatives of the people, is injurious to their rights, and ought not to be exercised.

8. That in all capital or criminal prosecutions a man hath a right to demand the cause and nature of his accusation, to be confronted with the accusers and witnesses, to call for evidence in his favor, and to a speedy trial by an impartial jury of twelve men of his vicinage,[4] without whose unanimous consent he cannot be found guilty, nor can he be compelled to give evidence against himself; that no man be deprived of his liberty, except by the law of the land or the judgment of his peers.

9. That excessive bail ought not to be required, nor excessive fines imposed, nor cruel and unusual punishments inflicted.

10. That general warrants, whereby any officer or messenger may be commanded to search suspected places without evidence of a fact

---

[2] able to descend to an heir

[3] burdens

[4] living in the same area or neighborhood

committed, or to seize any person or persons not named, or whose offence is not particularly described and supported by evidence, are grievous and oppressive, and ought not to be granted.

11. That in controversies respecting property, and in suits between man and man, the ancient trial by jury is preferable to any other, and ought to be held sacred.

12. That the freedom of the press is one of the great bulwarks of liberty, and can never be restrained but by despotic governments.

13. That a well regulated militia, composed of the body of the people, trained to arms, is the proper, natural, and safe defense of a free state; that standing armies, in time of peace, should be avoided, as dangerous to liberty; and that, in all cases, the military should be under strict subordination to, and governed by, the civil power.

14. That the people have a right to uniform government; and therefore, that no government separate from, or independent of, the government of Virginia, ought to be erected or established within the limits thereof.

15. That no free government, or the blessing of liberty, can be preserved to any people, but by a firm adherence to justice, moderation, temperance, frugality, and virtue, and by frequent recurrence to fundamental principles.

16. That religion, or the duty which we owe to our CREATOR, and the manner of discharging it, can be directed only by reason and conviction, not by force or violence, and therefore all men are equally entitled to the free exercise of religion, according to the dictates of conscience; and that it is the mutual duty of all to practice Christian forbearance, love, and charity, towards each other.

Virginia Constitution

The CONSTITUTION or FORM of GOVERNMENT, agreed to and resolved upon by the delegates and representatives of the several counties and corporations of Virginia.

I. WHEREAS George the third, King of Great Britain and Ireland, and elector of Hanover, heretofore entrusted with the exercise of the kingly office in this government, hath endeavored to pervert the same into a detestable and insupportable tyranny, by putting his negative on laws the most wholesome and necessary for the public good;

By denying his governors permission to pass laws of immediate and pressing importance, unless suspended in their operation for his assent, and, when so suspended, neglecting to attend to them for many years;

By refusing to pass certain other laws, unless the persons to be benefitted by them would relinquish the inestimable right of representation in the legislature;

By dissolving legislative assemblies repeatedly and continually, for opposing with manly firmness his invasions of the rights of the people;

When dissolved, by refusing to call others for a long space of time, thereby leaving the political system without any legislative head;

By endeavoring to prevent the population of our country, and, for that purpose, obstructing the laws for the naturalization of foreigners;

By keeping among us, in times of peace, standing armies and ships of war;

By affecting to render the military independent of, and superior to, the civil power;

By combining with others to subject us to a foreign jurisdiction, giving his assent to their pretended acts of legislation;

For quartering large bodies of armed troops among us;

For cutting off our trade with all parts of the world;

For imposing taxes on us, without our consent;

For depriving us of the benefits of trial by jury;

For transporting us beyond seas, to be tried for pretended offences;

For suspending our own legislatures, and declaring themselves invested with power to legislate for us in all cases whatsoever;

By plundering our seas, ravaging our coasts, burning our towns, and destroying the lives of our people;

By inciting insurrections of our fellow subjects, with the allurements of forfeiture and confiscation;

By prompting our negroes to rise in arms among us, those very negroes whom, by an inhuman use of his negative, he hath refused us permission to exclude by law;

By endeavoring to bring on the inhabitants of our frontiers the merciless Indian savages, whose known rule of warfare is an undistinguished destruction of all ages, sexes, and conditions of existence;

By transporting, at this time, a large army of foreign mercenaries, to complete the works of death, desolation, and tyranny, already begun with circumstances of cruelty and perfidy unworthy the head of a civilized nation;

By answering our repeated petitions for redress with a repetition of injuries;

And finally, by abandoning the helm of government, and declaring us out of his allegiance and protection.

By which several acts of misrule, the government of this country, as formerly exercised under the crown of Great Britain, is TOTALLY DISSOLVED.

II. We therefore, the delegates and representatives of the good people of Virginia, having maturely considered the premises, and viewing with great concern the deplorable condition to which this once happy country must be reduced, unless some regular, adequate mode of civil polity is speedily adopted, and in compliance with a recommendation of the General Congress, do ordain and declare the future form of government of Virginia to be as follows:

III. The legislative, executive, and judiciary departments, shall be separate and distinct, so that neither exercise the powers properly belonging to the other; nor shall any person exercise the powers of more than one of them at the same time, except that the justices of the county courts shall be eligible to either house of assembly.

IV. The legislative shall be formed of two distinct branches, who, together, shall be a complete legislature. They shall meet once, or oftener, every year, and shall be called the GENERAL ASSEMBLY OF VIRGINIA.

V. One of these shall be called the HOUSE OF DELEGATES, and consist of two representatives to be chosen for each county, and for the District of West-Augusta, annually, of such men as actually reside in, and are freeholders of the same, or duly qualified according to law, and also of one delegate or representative to be chosen annually for the city of Williamsburg, and one for the borough of Norfolk, and a representative for each of such other cities and boroughs as may hereafter be allowed particular representation by the legislature; but when any city or borough shall so decrease as that the number of persons having right of suffrage therein shall have been for the space of seven years successively less than half the number of voters in some one county in Virginia, such city or borough thenceforward shall cease to send a delegate or representative to the Assembly.

VI. The other shall be called the SENATE, and consist of twenty-four members, of whom thirteen shall constitute a House to proceed on business, for whose election the different counties shall be divided into twenty-four districts, and each county of the respective district, at the time of the election of its delegates, shall vote for one senator, who is actually a resident and freeholder within the district, or duly qualified according to law, and is upwards of twenty-five years of age; and the sheriffs of each county within five days at farthest after the last county election in the district, shall meet at some convenient place, and from the poll so taken in their respective counties return as a senator the man who shall have the greatest number of votes in the whole district. To keep up this assembly by rotation, the districts shall be equally divided into four classes, and numbered by lot. At the end of one year after the general election, the six members elected by the first division shall be displaced, and the vacancies thereby occasioned supplied from such class or division, by new election, in the manner aforesaid. This rotation shall be applied to each division, according to its number, and continued in due order annually.

VII. The right of suffrage in the election of members for both houses shall remain as exercised at present, and each house shall choose its own speaker, appoint its own officers, settle its own rules of proceeding, and direct writs of election for supplying intermediate vacancies.

VIII. All laws shall originate in the House of Delegates, to be approved or rejected by the Senate, or to be amended with the consent of the House of Delegates; except money bills, which in no instance shall be altered by the Senate, but wholly approved or rejected.

IX. A Governor, or chief magistrate, shall be chosen annually, by joint ballot of both Houses, to be taken in each house respectively, deposited in the conference room, the boxes examined jointly by a committee of each house, and the numbers severally reported to them, that the appointments may be entered (which shall be the mode of taking the joint ballot of both in all cases) who shall not continue in that office longer than three years successively, nor be eligible until the expiration of four years after he shall have been out of that office. An adequate, but moderate salary, shall be settled on him during his continuance in office; and he shall, with the advice of a Council of State, exercise the executive powers of government according to the laws of this commonwealth; and shall not, under any pretense, exercise any power or prerogative by virtue of any law, statute, or custom, of England: But he shall, with the advice of the Council of State, have the power of granting reprieves or pardons, except where the prosecution shall have been carried on by the House of Delegates, or the law shall otherwise particularly direct; in which cases, no reprieve or pardon shall be granted, but by resolve of the House of Delegates.

X. Either house of the General Assembly may adjourn themselves respectively. The Governor shall not prorogue[5] or adjourn the assembly during their sitting, nor dissolve them at any time; but he shall, if necessary, either

---

[5] discontinue or postpone the meetings of

by advice of the Council of State, or on application of a majority of the House of Delegates, call them before the time to which they shall stand prorogued or adjourned.

XI. A Privy Council, or Council of State, consisting of eight members, shall be chosen by joint ballot of both houses of assembly, either from their own members or the people at large, to assist in the administration of government. They shall annually choose out of their own members a president, who, in case of the death, inability, or necessary absence of the Governor from the government, shall act as Lieutenant Governor. Four members shall be sufficient to act, and their advice and proceedings shall be entered on record; and signed by the members present (to any part whereof any member may enter his dissent) to be laid before the General Assembly, when called for by them. This council may appoint their own clerk, who shall have a salary settled by law, and take an oath of secrecy in such matters as he shall be directed by the board to conceal. A sum of money appropriated to that purpose shall be divided annually among the members, in proportion to their attendance; and they shall be incapable, during their continuance in office, of sitting in either house of assembly. Two members shall be removed by joint ballot of both houses of assembly at the end of every three years, and be ineligible for the three next years. These vacancies, as well as those occasioned by death or incapacity, shall be supplied by new elections, in the same manner.

XII. The delegates for Virginia to the Continental Congress shall be chosen annually, or superseded in the mean time by joint ballot of both houses of assembly.

XIII. The present militia officers shall be continued, and vacancies supplied by appointment of the Governor, with the advice of the Privy Council, or recommendations from the respective county courts; but the Governor and Council shall have a power of suspending any officer, and ordering a court-martial on complaint for misbehavior or inability, or to supply vacancies of officers happening when in actual service. The governor may embody the militia, with the advice of the Privy Council; and, when embodied, shall alone have the direction of the militia under the laws of the country.

XIV. The two houses of assembly shall, by joint ballot, appoint judges of the Supreme Court of Appeals, and General Court, judges in chancery, judges of admiralty, Secretary, and the Attorney General, to be commissioned by the Governor, and continue in office during good behavior. In case of death, incapacity, or resignation, the governor, with the advice of the Privy Council, shall appoint persons to succeed in office, to be approved or displaced by both houses. These officers shall have fixed and adequate salaries, and, together with all others holding lucrative offices, and all ministers of the Gospel of every denomination, be incapable of being elected members of either house of assembly, or the Privy Council.

XV. The Governor, with the advice of the Privy Council, shall appoint justices of the peace for the counties; and in case of vacancies, or a necessity of increasing the number hereafter, such appointments to be made upon the recommendation of the respective county courts. The present acting Secretary in Virginia, and clerks of all the county courts, shall continue in office. In case of vacancies, either by death, incapacity, or resignation, a secretary shall be appointed as before directed, and the clerks by the respective courts. The present and future clerks shall hold their offices during good behavior, to be judged of and determined in the General Court. The sheriffs and coroners shall be nominated by the respective courts, approved by the Governor, with the advice of the Privy Council, and commissioned by the Governor. The justices shall appoint constables, and all fees of the aforesaid officers be regulated by law.

XVI. The Governor, when he is out of office, and others offending against the state, either by maladministration, corruption, or other means by which the safety of the state may be endangered, shall be impeachable by the House of Delegates. Such impeachment to be prosecuted by the Attorney General, or such other person or persons as the house may appoint in the General Court, according to the laws of the land. If found guilty, he or they shall be either for ever disabled to hold any office under government, or removed from such office *pro tempore*,[6] or subjected to such pains or penalties as the laws shall direct.

XVII. If all, or any of the judges of the General Court, shall, on good grounds (to be judged of by the House of Delegates) be accused of any of the crimes or offences before-mentioned, such House of Delegates may, in like manner, impeach the judge or judges so accused, to be prosecuted in the Court of Appeals; and he or they, if found guilty, shall be punished in the same manner as is prescribed in the preceding clause.

XVIII. Commissions and grants shall run, In the name of the COMMONWEALTH of VIRGINIA, and bear test by the Governor with the seal of the commonwealth annexed. Writs shall run in the same manner, and bear test by the clerks of the several courts. Indictments shall conclude, against the peace and dignity of the commonwealth.

---

[6] temporarily

XIX. A treasurer shall be appointed annually, by joint ballot of both Houses.

XX. All escheats,[7] penalties, and forfeitures, heretofore going to the king, shall go to the commonwealth, save only such as the legislature may abolish, or otherwise provide for.

XXI. The territories contained within the charters erecting the colonies of Maryland, Pennsylvania, North and South Carolina, are hereby ceded, released, and for ever confirmed to the people of those colonies respectively, with all the rights of property, jurisdiction, and government, and all other rights whatsoever which might at any time heretofore have been claimed by Virginia, except the free navigation and use of the rivers Potowmack[8] and Pohomoke,[9] with the property of the Virginia shores or strands bordering on either of the said rivers, and all improvements which have been or shall be made thereon. The western and northern extent of Virginia shall in all other respects stand as fixed by the Charter of King James the first, in the year one thousand six hundred and nine, and by the public treaty of peace between the courts of Great Britain and France in the year one thousand seven hundred and sixty three; unless by act of legislature, one or more territories shall hereafter be laid off, and governments established westward of the Allegheny mountains. And no purchase of land shall be made of the Indian natives but on behalf of the public, by authority of the General Assembly.

XXII. In order to introduce this government, the representatives of the people met in convention shall choose a Governor and Privy Council, also such other officers directed to be chosen by both houses as may be judged necessary to be immediately appointed. The Senate to be first chosen by the people, to continue until the last day of March next, and the other officers until the end of the succeeding session of assembly. In case of vacancies, the speaker of either house shall issue writs for new elections.

---

[7] reversions of property in absence of a legal heir
[8] Potomac River
[9] Pocomoke River

The New Jersey Constitution

July 3, 1776

T he 1776 New Jersey Constitution, framed by a convention that met from May 26 through July 3, was the second to be adopted by the new states and the first to omit a prefatory bill of rights. Nevertheless, the constitution appeals to "the nature of things" and the American covenanting tradition. Moreover, civil rights and criminal procedures are addressed in four of the thirty-nine articles. The New Jersey model of incorporating a bill of rights in a constitution rather than the Virginia model (Document 3) of having a bill of rights outside the Constitution is revisited in the First Congress (Documents 22–25).

Article XVI of the New Jersey Constitution provides that "all criminals shall be admitted to the same privileges of witness and counsel, as their prosecutors do or shall be entitled to," and Article XXII confirms the common law tradition with the trial by jury being given permanent protection. Two articles address the issue of religious rights. Article XVIII guarantees to all "the inestimable privilege of worshipping Almighty God in a manner agreeable to the dictates of his own conscience," and proclaims that no one shall ever be obliged to support financially any ministry "contrary to what he believes to be right, or has deliberately or voluntarily engaged himself to perform." Article XIX states that there "shall be no establishment of any one religious sect in this Province, in preference to another," and that "all persons, professing a belief in the faith of any Protestant sect... shall fully and freely enjoy every privilege and immunity, enjoyed by others their fellow subjects." New Jersey was the first state to prohibit the establishment of a specific sect as the official religion.

SOURCE: *The Essential Bill of Rights*, ed. Gordon Lloyd and Margie Lloyd, (Lanham, MD: University Press of America, 1998), 196–201. We have followed F. N. Thorpe, *The Federal and State Constitutions* (Washington, DC: Government Printing Office, 1909) vol. V: 2594–2598; https://goo.gl/fzFbWj. The Roman numerals are in the original.

WHEREAS all the constitutional authority ever possessed by the kings of Great Britain over these colonies, or their other dominions, was, by compact, derived from the people, and held of them, for the common interest of the whole society; allegiance and protection are, in the nature of things, reciprocal ties, each equally depending upon the other, and liable to be dissolved by the others being refused or withdrawn. And whereas George the Third, king of Great Britain, has refused protection to the good people of these colonies; and, by assenting to sundry acts of the British Parliament, attempted to subject them to the absolute dominion of that body; and has also made war upon them, in the most cruel and unnatural manner, for no other cause, than asserting their just rights—all civil authority under him is necessarily at an end, and a dissolution of government in each colony has consequently taken place.

And whereas, in the present deplorable situation of these colonies, exposed to the fury of a cruel and relentless enemy, some form of government is absolutely necessary, not only for the preservation of good order, but also the more effectually to unite the people, and enable them to exert their whole force in their own necessary defense: and as the honorable the continental congress, the supreme council of the American colonies, has advised such of the colonies as have not yet gone into measures, to adopt for themselves, respectively, such government as shall best conduce to their own happiness and safety, and the well-being of America in general: We, the representatives of the colony of New Jersey, having been elected by all the counties, in the freest manner, and in congress assembled, have, after mature deliberations, agreed upon a set of charter rights and the form of a constitution, in manner following, viz.

I. That the government of this province shall be vested in a Governor, Legislative Council, and General Assembly.

II. That the Legislative Council, and General Assembly, shall be chosen, for the first time, on the second Tuesday in August next; the members whereof shall be the same in number and qualifications as are herein after mentioned; and shall be and remain vested with all the powers and authority to be held by any future Legislative Council and Assembly of this colony, until the second Tuesday in October, which shall be in the year of our Lord one thousand seven hundred and seventy-seven.

III. That on the second Tuesday in October yearly, and every year forever (with the privilege of adjourning from day to day as occasion may require) the counties shall severally choose one person, to be a member of the Legislative Council of this colony, who shall be, and have been, for one whole year next before the election, an inhabitant and freeholder in the county in which he is chosen, and worth at least one thousand pounds proclamation money,[1] of real and personal estate, within the same county; that, at the same time, each county shall also choose three members of assembly; provided that no person shall be entitled to a seat in the said assembly unless he be, and have been, for one whole year next before the election, an inhabitant of the county he is to represent, and worth five hundred pounds proclamation money, in real and personal estate, in the same county: that on the second Tuesday next after the day of election, the council and assembly shall separately meet; and that the consent of both houses shall be necessary to every law; provided, that seven shall be a quorum of the council, for doing business, and that no law shall pass, unless there be a majority of all the representatives of each body personally present, and agreeing thereto. Provided always, that if a majority of the representatives of this province, in council and General Assembly convened, shall, at any time or times hereafter, judge it equitable and proper, to add to or diminish the number or proportion of the members of assembly for any county or counties in this colony, then, and in such case, the same may, on the principles of more equal representation, be lawfully done; anything in this charter to the contrary notwithstanding: so that the whole number of representatives in assembly shall not, at any time, be less than thirty-nine.

IV. That all inhabitants of this colony, of full age, who are worth fifty pounds proclamation money, clear estate in the same, and have resided within the county in which they claim a vote for twelve months immediately preceding the election, shall be entitled to vote for representatives in council and assembly; and also for all other public officers, that shall be elected by the people of the county at large.

V. That the assembly, when met, shall have power to choose a speaker, and other their officers; to be judges of the qualifications and elections of their own members; sit upon their own adjournments; prepare bills, to be passed into laws; and to empower their speaker to convene them, whenever any extraordinary occurrence shall render it necessary.

VI. That the council shall also have power to prepare bills to pass into laws, and have other like powers as the Assembly, and in all respects be a free and independent branch of the legislature of this colony; save only, that they shall not prepare or alter any money bill—which shall be the privilege of the assembly; that the council shall, from time to time, be convened by the Governor or Vice President, but must be convened, at all times, when

---

[1] A proclamation in 1704 by Queen Anne attempted to regulate coinage in the colonies. Coinage so regulated was known as proclamation money.

the Assembly sits; for which purpose the speaker of the House of Assembly shall always, immediately after an adjournment, give notice to the Governor, or Vice President, of the time and place to which the House is adjourned.

VII. That the council and assembly jointly, at their first meeting after each annual election, shall, by a majority of votes, elect some fit person within the colony, to be Governor for one year, who shall be constant president of the Council, and have a casting vote in their proceedings; and that the council themselves shall choose a Vice President who shall act as such in the absence of the Governor.

VIII. That the Governor, or, in his absence, the Vice President of the council, shall have the supreme executive power, be chancellor of the colony, and act as captain-general and commander in chief of all the militia, and other military force in this colony; and that any three or more of the council shall, at all times, be a privy-council, to consult them; and that the Governor be ordinary or surrogate-general.

IX. That the Governor and council, (seven whereof shall be a quorum) be the court of appeals, in the last resort, in all clauses of law, as heretofore; and that they possess the power of granting pardons to criminals, after condemnation, in all cases of treason, felony, or other offences.

X. That captains, and all other inferior officers of the militia, shall be chosen by the companies, in the respective counties; but field and general officers, by the council and assembly.

XI. That the council and assembly shall have power to make the Great Seal of this Colony, which shall be kept by the Governor, or, in his absence, by the Vice President of the council, to be used by them as occasion may require: and it shall be called, the Great Seal of the Colony of New-Jersey.

XII. That the judges of the Supreme Court shall continue in office for seven years: the judges of the Inferior Court of Common Pleas in the several counties, justices of the peace, clerks of the Supreme Court, clerks of the Inferior Court of Common Pleas and Quarter Sessions,[2] the Attorney General, and provincial Secretary, shall continue in office for five years: and the provincial Secretary shall continue in office for one year; and that they shall be severally appointed by the council and assembly, in manner aforesaid, and commissioned by the Governor, or, in his absence, the Vice President of the council. Provided always, that the said officers, severally, shall be capable of being re-appointed, at the end of the terms severally before limited; and that

---

[2] A lower local court hearing cases involving smaller amounts of money or property and some less serious civil and criminal complaints

any of the said officers shall be liable to be dismissed, when adjudged guilty of misbehavior, by the council, on an impeachment of the assembly.

XIII. That the inhabitants of each county, qualified to vote as aforesaid, shall at the time and place of electing their Representatives, annually elect one sheriff, and one or more coroners; and that they may re-elect the same person to such offices, until he shall have served three years, but no longer; after which, three years must elapse before the same person is capable of being elected again. When the election is certified to the Governor, or Vice President, under the hands of six freeholders[3] of the county for which they were elected, they shall be immediately commissioned to serve in their respective offices.

XIV. That the townships, at their annual town meetings for electing other officers, shall choose constables for the districts respectively; and also three or more judicious freeholders of good character, to hear and finally determine all appeals, relative to unjust assessments, in cases of public taxation; which commissioners of appeal shall, for that purpose, sit at some suitable time or times, to be by them appointed, and made known to the people by advertisements.

XV. That the laws of the colony shall begin in the following style, viz. "Be it enacted by the council and General Assembly of this colony, and it is hereby enacted by authority of the same:" that all commissions, granted by the Governor or Vice President, shall run thus—"The Colony of New Jersey to A. B. &c. greeting:" and that all writs shall likewise run in the name of the Colony: and that all indictments shall conclude in the following manner, viz. "Against the peace of this colony, the government and dignity of the same."

XVI. That all criminals shall be admitted to the same privileges of witnesses and counsel, as their prosecutors are or shall be entitled to.

XVII. That the estates of such persons as shall destroy their own lives, shall not, for that offence, be forfeited; but shall descend in the same manner, as they would have done, had such persons died in the natural way; nor shall any article, which may occasion accidentally the death of any one, be henceforth deemed a deodand,[4] or in anywise forfeited, on account of such misfortune.

XVIII. That no person shall ever, within this colony, be deprived of the inestimable privilege of worshipping Almighty God in a manner agreeable to the dictates of his own conscience; nor, under any pretense whatever,

---

[3] A freeholder is someone who owns property without obligation to anyone else.
[4] Something forfeited because it caused the death of someone

be compelled to attend any place of worship, contrary to his own faith and judgment; nor shall any person, within this colony, ever be obliged to pay tithes, taxes, or any other rates, for the purpose of building or repairing any other church or churches, place or places of worship, or for the maintenance of any minister or ministry, contrary to what he believes to be right, or has deliberately or voluntarily engaged himself to perform.

XIX. That there shall be no establishment of any one religious sect in this province, in preference to another; and that no Protestant inhabitant of this colony shall be denied the enjoyment of any civil right, merely on account of his religious principles; but that all persons, professing a belief in the faith of any Protestant sect, who shall demean themselves peaceably under the government, as hereby established, shall be capable of being elected into any office of profit or trust, or being a member of either branch of the legislature, and shall fully and freely enjoy every privilege and immunity, enjoyed by others their fellow subjects.

XX. That the legislative department of this government may, as much as possible, be preserved from all suspicion of corruption, none of the Judges of the supreme or other courts, sheriffs, or any other person or persons possessed of any post of profit under the government, other than justices of the peace, shall be entitled to a seat in the assembly: but that, on his being elected, and taking his seat, his office or post shall be considered as vacant.

XXI. That all the laws of this province, contained in the edition lately published by Mr. Allinson,[5] shall be and remain in full force, until altered by the legislature of this colony (such only excepted, as are incompatible with this charter) and shall be, according as heretofore, regarded in all respects, by all civil officers, and others, the good people of this province.

XXII. That the common law of England, as well as so much of the statute law, as have been heretofore practiced in this colony, shall still remain in force, until they shall be altered by a future law of the legislature; such parts only excepted, as are repugnant to the rights and privileges contained in this charter; and that the inestimable right of trial by jury shall remain confirmed as a part of the laws of this colony, without repeal, forever.

XXIII. That every person, who shall be elected as aforesaid to be a member

---

[5] Samuel Allinson (1739–1791), a Quaker, was an attorney commissioned by the New Jersey legislature in 1773 to prepare a compilation of the laws of New Jersey. The compilation was published in 1776. See *Documents Relating to the Revolutionary History of the State of New Jersey*, edited by William A. Stryker (Trenton, NJ: the John L. Murphy Publishing Company, 1901), 63.

of the Legislative Council, or House of Assembly, shall, previous to this taking his seat in council or assembly, take the following oath or affirmation, viz:

"I, A. B., do solemnly declare, that, as a member of the Legislative Council, (or Assembly, as the case may be,) of the Colony of New Jersey, I will not assent to any law, vote or proceeding, which shall appear to me injurious to the public welfare of said colony, nor that shall annul or repeal that part of the third section in the charter of this colony, which establishes, that the elections of members of the Legislative Council and Assembly shall be annual; nor that part of the twenty-second section in said charter, respecting the trial by jury, nor that shall annul, repeal, or alter any part or parts of the eighteenth or nineteenth sections of the same."

And any person or persons, who shall be elected as aforesaid, is hereby empowered to administer to the said members the said oath or affirmation.

Provided always, and it is the true intent and meaning of this Congress, that if a reconciliation between Great Britain and these colonies should take place, and the latter be taken again under the protection and government of the crown of Britain, this charter shall be null and void—otherwise to remain firm and inviolable.

In Provincial Congress, New Jersey,
Burlington, July 2, 1776.

By order of Congress. SAMUEL TUCKER, Pres.
WILLIAM PATTERSON, Secretary

The Pennsylvania Declaration of Rights and Constitution

September 28, 1776

The Pennsylvania Constitution, prefaced by a Preamble and Declaration of Rights, was framed by a specially elected convention that met from mid-July to the end of September 1776. Pennsylvania followed the Virginia model of declaring a bill of rights prior to articulating the kind of republican government that will be established (Document 3).

Although the Pennsylvania document was not submitted to the people for ratification, it expresses the radical populist dimension of the conversation over what frame of government would best secure the rights of the people: Pennsylvania was the only state to choose a unicameral rather than a bicameral legislature. Although the legislature was very powerful, the constitution calls for an "open" assembly with policymaking taking place under the full scrutiny of an informed electorate. In section forty-seven (omitted below), the Pennsylvania Constitution provided for an elected Council of Censors to provide periodic review of the operation of the laws and institutions "in order that the freedom of the commonwealth may be preserved inviolate for ever." This model was subsequently praised by Thomas Jefferson in his Notes on the State of Virginia and criticized by James Madison in The Federalist, numbers 47–51.

John Adams's 1779 judgment that the Pennsylvania Bill of Rights "is taken almost verbatim from that of Virginia" is correct as far as it concerns the common law tradition. Nevertheless, all sixteen rights enunciated in the Bill of Rights deserve to be reproduced in their entirety in order to appreciate the remarkable uniformity and subtle differences among the states. It is particularly important to note that Pennsylvania repeats the claim that "a firm adherence to justice, moderation, temperance, industry, and frugality are absolutely necessary to preserve the blessings of liberty," and that only Christians are eligible to hold office. Also noteworthy are the sections dealing with searches and seizures, freedom of speech, the right to bear arms, "the natural inherent right to emigrate," and the right to assemble.

For organizational purposes, we have divided the text into two parts. Part 1 contains a preamble. Part 2 lists sixteen "rights." The Roman numerals are in the *original text. A Part 3 would have reproduced the forty-seven sections of the plan of government in the Constitution. The plan is omitted.*

SOURCE: *The Essential Bill of Rights*, ed. Gordon Lloyd and Margie Lloyd, (Lanham, MD: University Press of America,1998), 202–215. We have followed F. N. Thorpe, *The Federal and State Constitutions* (Washington, DC: Washington: Government Printing Office, 1909), vol. 5: 3081-3092; https://goo.gl/gMQuJj. We have followed the spelling, abbreviations, and punctuation found in Thorpe's version.

[Part 1: Preamble]

WHEREAS all government ought to be instituted and supported for the security and protection of the community as such, and to enable the individuals who compose it to enjoy their natural rights, and the other blessings which the Author of existence has bestowed upon man; and whenever these great ends of government are not obtained, the people have a right, by common consent to change it, and take such measures as to them may appear necessary to promote their safety and happiness. AND WHEREAS the inhabitants of this commonwealth have in consideration of protection only, heretofore acknowledged allegiance to the king of Great Britain; and the said king has not only withdrawn that protection, but commenced, and still continues to carry on, with unabated vengeance, a most cruel and unjust war against them, employing therein, not only the troops of Great Britain, but foreign mercenaries, savages and slaves, for the avowed purpose of reducing them to a total and abject submission to the despotic domination of the British parliament, with many other acts of tyranny, (more fully set forth in the declaration of Congress)[1] whereby all allegiance and fealty to the said king and his successors, are dissolved and at an end, and all power and authority derived from him ceased in these colonies. AND WHEREAS it is absolutely necessary for the welfare and safety of the inhabitants of said colonies, that they be henceforth free and independent States, and that just, permanent, and proper forms of government exist in every part of them, derived from and founded on the authority of the people only, agreeable to the directions of the honorable American Congress. We, the representatives of the freemen of Pennsylvania, in general convention met, for the express purpose of framing such a government, confessing the goodness of the great Governor of the

---

[1] Declaration of Independence

universe (who alone knows to what degree of earthly happiness mankind may attain, by perfecting the arts of government) in permitting the people of this State, by common consent, and without violence, deliberately to form for themselves such just rules as they shall think best, for governing their future society; and being fully convinced, that it is our indispensable duty to establish such original principles of government, as will best promote the general happiness of the people of this State, and their posterity, and provide for future improvements, without partiality for, or prejudice against any particular class, sect, or denomination of men whatever, do, by virtue of the authority vested in us by our constituents, ordain, declare, and establish, the following Declaration of Rights and Frame of Government, to be the CONSTITUTION of this commonwealth, and to remain in force therein for ever, unaltered, except in such articles as shall hereafter on experience be found to require improvement, and which shall by the same authority of the people, fairly delegated as this frame of government directs, be amended or improved for the more effectual obtaining and securing the great end and design of all government, herein before mentioned.

[Part 2: Bill of Rights]

A Declaration of the Rights of the Inhabitants of the Commonwealth, or State of Pennsylvania

I. That all men are born equally free and independent, and have certain natural, inherent and inalienable rights, amongst which are, the enjoying and defending life and liberty, acquiring, possessing and protecting property, and pursuing and obtaining happiness and safety.

II. That all men have a natural and unalienable right to worship Almighty God according to the dictates of their own consciences and understanding: And that no man ought or of right can be compelled to attend any religious worship, or erect or support any place of worship, or maintain any ministry, contrary to, or against, his own free will and consent: Nor can any man, who acknowledges the being of a God, be justly deprived or abridged of any civil right as a citizen, on account of his religious sentiments or peculiar mode of religious worship: And that no authority can or ought to be vested in, or assumed by any power whatever, that shall in any case interfere with, or in any manner control, the right of conscience in the free exercise of religious worship.

III. That the people of this state have the sole, exclusive and inherent right of governing and regulating the internal police of the same.

IV. That all power being originally inherent in, and consequently derived from, the people; therefore all officers of government, whether legislative or executive, are their trustees and servants, and at all time accountable to them.

V. That government is, or ought to be, instituted for the common benefit, protection and security of the people, nation or community; and not for the particular emolument or advantage of any single man, family, or set of men, who are a part only of that community; And that the community hath an indubitable, unalienable and indefeasible right to reform, alter, or abolish government in such manner as shall be by that community judged most conducive to the public weal.

VI. That those who are employed in the legislative and executive business of the state, may be restrained from oppression, the people have a right, at such periods as they may think proper, to reduce their public officers to a private station, and supply the vacancies by certain and regular elections.

VII. That all elections ought to be free; and that all free men having a sufficient evident common interest with, and attachment to the community, have a right to elect officers, or to be elected into office.

VIII. That every member of society hath a right to be protected in the enjoyment of life, liberty and property, and therefore is bound to contribute his proportion towards the expense of that protection, and yield his personal service when necessary, or an equivalent thereto: But no part of a man's property can be justly taken from him, or applied to public uses, without his own consent, or that of his legal representatives: Nor can any man who is conscientiously scrupulous of bearing arms, be justly compelled thereto, if he will pay such equivalent, nor are the people bound by any laws, but such as they have in like manner assented to, for their common good.

IX. That in all prosecutions for criminal offences, a man hath a right to be heard by himself and his council, to demand the cause and nature of his accusation, to be confronted with the witnesses, to call for evidence in his favor, and a speedy public trial, by an impartial jury of the country, without the unanimous consent of which jury he cannot be found guilty; nor can he be compelled to give evidence against himself; nor can any man be justly deprived of his liberty except by the laws of the land, or the judgment of his peers.

X. That the people have a right to hold themselves, their houses, papers, and possessions free from search and seizure, and therefore warrants without oaths or affirmations first made, affording a sufficient foundation for them, and whereby any officer or messenger may be commanded or required to search suspected places, or to seize any person or persons, his or their property, not particularly described, are contrary to that right, and ought not to be granted.

XI. That in controversies respecting property, and in suits between man and man, the parties have a right to trial by jury, which ought to be held sacred.

XII. That the people have a right to freedom of speech, and of writing, and publishing their sentiments; therefore the freedom of the press ought not to be restrained.

XIII. That the people have a right to bear arms for the defense of themselves and the state; and as standing armies in the time of peace are dangerous to liberty, they ought not to be kept up; And that the military should be kept under strict subordination to, and governed by, the civil power.

XIV. That a frequent recurrence to fundamental principles, and a firm adherence to justice, moderation, temperance, industry, and frugality are absolutely necessary to preserve the blessings of liberty, and keep a government free: The people ought therefore to pay particular attention to these points in the choice of officers and representatives, and have a right to exact a due and constant regard to them, from their legislatures and magistrates, in the making and executing such laws as are necessary for the good government of the state.

XV. That all men have a natural inherent right to emigrate from one state to another that will receive them, or to form a new state in vacant countries, or in such countries as they can purchase, whenever they think that thereby they may promote their own happiness.

XVI. That the people have a right to assemble together, to consult for their common good, to instruct their representatives, and to apply to the legislature for redress of grievances, by address, petition, or remonstrance.

The Massachusetts Declaration of Rights and Constitution

March 2, 1780

The Massachusetts Declaration of Rights and Constitution was adopted by a convention March 2, 1780 and approved by the votes of the people June 15, 1780. It was the first state constitution to be ratified by the people directly rather than by the people's representatives. This became the model for the adoption of the U.S. Constitution. This 1780 Constitution was a revised version of the 1778 Constitution rejected because of the absence of a Bill of Rights, the absence of popular ratification, and the denial of the right of suffrage to free "negroes, Indians, and mulattoes." The Massachusetts Constitution of 1780 is the oldest written constitution in continuous effect.

The Massachusetts Preamble confirmed the "right of the people to set up what government they believe will secure their safety, prosperity, and happiness." The provisions in "Part the First" dealing with search and seizure, self-incrimination, confrontation of witnesses, self-incrimination, cruel and unusual punishments, freedom of press, the right to petition, and that no one shall be deprived of "life, liberty, or estate, but by the judgment of his peers, or the law of the land," were common among all the states that adopted a bill of rights. Massachusetts also included specific political rights of the people: the right to be free of ex post facto laws, to frequent elections, to an independent judiciary, and to a strict separation of governmental powers "to the end that it may be a government of laws and not of men."

Following Virginia and Pennsylvania (Documents 3 and 5), the need for "piety, justice, moderation, temperance, industry, and frugality" was listed in the Bill of Rights. What is distinctive about Massachusetts is that the virtue of the people was to be secured by established religion. The third "right" was that of the citizens to support, financially, the establishment of public religion. No one particular sect was given preference over another; all were "equally under the protection of the law"—hence the claim that the "free exercise" of religion was protected. Thus the debate over freedom of conscience and the establishment of religion was persistent between 1776 and 1780.

SOURCE: *The Essential Bill of Rights*, ed. Gordon Lloyd and Margie Lloyd, (Lanham, MD: University Press of America, 1998), 218–224. We have followed F. N. Thorpe, *The Federal and State Constitutions* (Washington, DC: Government Printing Office, 1909) Vol. 3:1888–1893; https://goo.gl/ZUzBVe. The Roman numerals are in the original.

A Constitution or Form of Government for the Commonwealth of Massachusetts

Preamble

The end of the institution, maintenance, and administration of government, is to secure the existence of the body politic, to protect it, and to furnish the individuals, who compose it, with the power of enjoying, in safety and tranquility, their natural rights, and the blessings of life: and whenever these great objects are not obtained, the people have a right to alter the government, and to take measures, necessary for their safety, prosperity, and happiness.

The body politic is formed by a voluntary association of individuals. It is a social compact, by which the whole people covenants with each citizen, and each citizen with the whole people, that all shall be governed by certain laws for the common good. It is the duty of the people, therefore, in framing a constitution of government, to provide for an equitable mode of making laws, as well as for an impartial interpretation, and a faithful execution of them; that every man may, at all times, find his security in them.

We, therefore, the people of Massachusetts, acknowledging, with grateful hearts, the goodness of the Great Legislator of the Universe, in affording us, in the course of his providence, an opportunity, deliberately and peaceably, without fraud, violence or surprise, of entering into an original, explicit, and solemn compact with each other; and of forming a new constitution of government, for ourselves and posterity; and devoutly imploring His direction in so interesting a design, do agree upon, ordain, and establish, the following Declaration of Rights, and Frame of Government, as the Constitution of the Commonwealth of Massachusetts.

Part the First: A Declaration of the Rights of the Inhabitants of the Commonwealth of Massachusetts

Article I. All men are born free and equal, and have certain natural, essential, and unalienable rights; among which may be reckoned the right of enjoying and defending their lives and liberties; that of acquiring, possessing, and protecting property; in fine, that of seeking and obtaining their safety and happiness.

II. It is the right, as well as the duty of all men in society, publicly, and at stated seasons, to worship the Supreme Being, the great Creator and Preserver of the Universe. And no subject shall be hurt, molested, or restrained, in his person, liberty, or estate, for worshipping God, in the manner and season, most agreeable to the dictates of his own conscience; or for his religious profession or sentiments; provided he doth not disturb the public peace, or obstruct others in their religious worship.

III. As the happiness of a people, and the good order and preservation of civil government, essentially depend upon piety, religion, and morality; and as these cannot be generally diffused through a community, but by the institution of the public worship of God, and of public instructions in piety, religion, and morality: Therefore, to promote their happiness, and to secure the good order and preservation of their government, the people of this commonwealth have a right to invest their legislature with power to authorize and require, and the legislature shall, from time to time, authorize and require, the several towns, parishes, precincts, and other bodies politic, or religious societies, to make suitable provision at their own expense, for the institution of the public worship of God, and for the support and maintenance of public protestant teachers of piety, religion, and morality, in all cases, where such provision shall not be made voluntarily.

And the people of this commonwealth have also a right to, and do, invest their legislature with authority, to enjoin, upon all the subjects, an attendance upon the instructions of the public teachers aforesaid, at stated times and seasons, if there be any, on whose instructions they can conscientiously, and conveniently attend.

Provided, notwithstanding, that the several towns, parishes, precincts, and other bodies politic, or religious societies, shall, at all times, have the exclusive right of electing their public teachers, and of contracting with them, for their support and maintenance.

And all monies, paid by the subject to the support of public worship, and of the public teachers aforesaid, shall, if he require it, be uniformly applied to the support of the public teacher or teachers, of his own religious sect or denomination, provided there be any, on whose instructions he attends; otherwise it may be paid towards the support of the teacher or teachers, of the parish, or precinct, in which the said monies are raised.

And every denomination of Christians, demeaning themselves peaceably, and as good subjects of the commonwealth, shall be equally under the protection of the law: and no subordination of any one sect or denomination, to another, shall ever be established by law.

IV. The people of this commonwealth have the sole and exclusive right of governing themselves, as a free, sovereign, and independent state; and do, and forever hereafter shall, exercise and enjoy every power, jurisdiction, and right, which is not, or may not hereafter be, by them expressly delegated to the United States of America, in Congress assembled.

V. All power residing originally in the people, and being derived from them, the several magistrates, and officers of government, vested with authority, whether legislative, executive, or judicial, are their substitutes and agents, and are at all times accountable to them.

VI. No man, or corporation, or association of men, have any other title, to obtain advantages, or particular and exclusive privileges, distinct from those of the community, than what arises from the consideration of services rendered to the public. And this title being in nature, neither hereditary, nor transmissible to children, or descendants, or relations by blood, the idea of a man born a magistrate, lawgiver, or judge, is absurd and unnatural.

VII. Government is instituted for the common good; for the protection, safety, prosperity, and happiness of the people; and not for the profit, honor, or private interest of any one man, family, or class of men: Therefore, the people alone have an incontestable, unalienable, and indefeasible right, to institute government; and to reform, alter, or totally change the same, when their protection, safety, prosperity and happiness, require it.

VIII. In order to prevent those, who are vested with authority, from becoming oppressors, the people have a right, at such periods, and in such manner, as they shall establish by their frame of government, to cause their public officers to return to private life; and to fill up vacant places by certain and regular elections and appointments.

IX. All elections ought to be free; and all the inhabitants of this commonwealth, having such qualifications, as they shall establish by their frame of government, have an equal right to elect officers, and to be elected, for public employments.

X. Each individual of the society has a right to be protected by it, in the enjoyment of his life, liberty, and property, according to standing laws. He is obliged, consequently, to contribute his share to the expense of this protection; to give his personal service, or an equivalent, when necessary. But no part of the property of any individual can, with justice, be taken from him, or applied to public uses, without his own consent, or that of the representative body of the people. In fine, the people of this commonwealth are not controllable by any other laws, than those to which their constitutional representative body have given their consent. And whenever the public exigencies require, that the property of any individual should be appropriated to public uses, he shall receive a reasonable compensation therefore.

XI. Every subject of the commonwealth ought to find a certain remedy, by having recourse to the laws, for all injuries or wrongs, which he may receive, in his person, property, or character. He ought to obtain right and justice freely, and without being obliged to purchase it; completely, and without any denial; promptly, and without delay; conformably to the laws.

XII. No subject shall be held to answer for any crimes or offense, until the same is fully and plainly, substantially and formally, described to him; or be compelled to accuse, or furnish evidence against himself. And every subject shall have a right to produce all proofs that may be favorable to him; to meet the witnesses against him, face to face; and to be fully heard in his defense, by himself, or his council, at his election. And no subject shall be arrested, imprisoned, despoiled, or deprived of his property, immunities, or privileges, put out of the protection of the law, exiled, or deprived of his life, liberty, or estate, but by the judgment of his peers, or the law of the land.

And the legislature shall not make any law, that shall subject any person to a capital or infamous punishment, excepting for the government of the army and navy, without trial by jury.

XIII. In criminal prosecutions, the verification of facts, in the vicinity where they happen, is one of the greatest securities of the life, liberty and property of the citizen.

XIV. Every subject has a right to be secure from all unreasonable searches, and seizures, of his person, his houses, his papers, and all his possessions. All warrants, therefore, are contrary to this right, if the cause or foundation of them be not previously supported by oath or affirmation, [or] if the order, in the warrant, to a civil officer, to make search in suspected places, or to arrest one or more suspected persons, or to seize their property, be not accompanied with a special designation of the persons or objects of search, arrest, or seizure; and no warrant ought to be issued, but in cases, and with the formalities, prescribed by the laws.

XV. In all controversies concerning property, and in all suits between two or more persons, except in cases in which it has heretofore been otherwise used and practiced, the parties have a right to a trial by jury; and this method of procedure shall be held sacred, unless, in causes arising on the high seas, and such as relate to mariners' wages, the Legislature shall hereafter find it necessary to alter it.

XVI. The liberty of the press is essential to the security of freedom in a state; it ought not, therefore, to be restrained in this commonwealth.

XVII. The people have a right to keep and to bear arms for the common defense. And as, in time of peace, armies are dangerous to liberty, they ought not to be maintained, without the consent of the legislature; and the military power shall always be held in an exact subordination to the civil authority, and be governed by it.

XVIII. A frequent recurrence to the fundamental principles of the Constitution, and a constant adherence to those of piety, justice, moderation, temperance, industry, and frugality, are absolutely necessary, to preserve the advantages of liberty, and to maintain a free government. The people ought, consequently, to have a particular attention to all those principles, in the choice of their officers and representatives: and they have a right to require of their lawgivers and magistrates, an exact and constant observance of them, in the formation and execution of the laws, necessary for the good administration of the Commonwealth.

XIX. The people have a right, in an orderly and peaceable manner, to assemble to consult upon the common good; give instructions to their representatives; and to request of the legislative body, by the way of addresses, petitions, or remonstrances, redress of the wrongs done them, and of the grievances they suffer.

XX. The power of suspending the laws, or the execution of the laws, ought never to be exercised, but by the legislature or, by authority derived from it, to be exercised in such particular cases only, as the legislature shall expressly provide for.

XXI. The freedom of deliberation, speech, and debate, in either house of the legislature, is so essential to the rights of the people, that it cannot be the foundation of any accusation, or prosecution, action, or complaint, in any other court or place whatsoever.

XXII. The legislature ought frequently to assemble, for the redress of grievances, for correcting, strengthening, and confirming the laws, and for making new laws, as the common good may require.

XXIII. No subsidy, charge, tax, impost, or duties, ought to be established, fixed, laid, or levied, under any pretext whatsoever, without the consent of the people, or their representatives in the legislature.

XXIV. Laws made to punish for actions done before the existence of such laws, and which have not been declared crimes by preceding laws, are unjust, oppressive, and inconsistent with the fundamental principles of a free government.

XXV. No subject ought, in any case, or in any time, to be declared guilty of treason or felony by the legislature.

XXVI. No magistrate, or court of law, shall demand excessive bail, or sureties, impose excessive fines, or inflict cruel or unusual punishments.

XXVII. In time of peace, no soldier ought to be quartered in any house, without the consent of the owner; and in time of war, such quarters ought not to be made, but by the civil magistrate, in a manner ordained by the legislature.

XXVIII. No person can, in any case, be subjected to law martial, or to any penalties or pains, by virtue of that law, except those employed in the army or navy, and except the militia, in actual service, but by authority of the legislature.

XXIX. It is essential to the preservation of the rights of every individual, his life, liberty, property, and character, that there be an impartial interpretation of the laws, and administration of justice. It is the right of every citizen, to be tried by judges, as free, impartial, and independent, as the lot of humanity will admit. It is, therefore, not only the best policy, but for the security of the rights of the people, and of every citizen, that the judges of the Supreme Judicial Court should hold their offices as long as they behave themselves well; and that they should have honorable salaries, ascertained and established by standing laws.

XXX. In the government of this commonwealth, the legislative department shall never exercise the executive and judicial powers, or either of them: the executive shall never exercise the legislative and judicial powers, or either of them: the judicial shall never exercise the legislative and executive powers, or either of them: to the end, it may be a government of laws, and not of men.

James Madison's Memorial and Remonstrance

June 20, 1785

Virginia entered unfamiliar territory with the disestablishment of the Anglican Church in 1779. Nevertheless, there were two competing models to which legislators could turn to sort out relations between church and state after disestablishment. The Massachusetts model endorsed the establishment of the Christian Protestant religion and, to that end, the legislature was constitutionally mandated to tax inhabitants for the support of public religious instruction (Document 6). The taxpayer, nevertheless, was free to name the specific religion that was to receive the assessment. On the other hand, the Pennsylvania model warned that such taxation threatened the right of an individual to the free exercise of religion. Pennsylvania had opted not to have the state support any church. In December 1784, the Virginia Assembly considered an assessment bill, consistent with the Massachusetts model, that would financially support the encouragement of Christianity as the state religion. Writing on behalf of a group who opposed this bill, James Madison addressed the Memorial and Remonstrance to the Virginia Assembly. He urged the legislators to reject the proposed legislation and in the process listed fifteen "becauses," or reasons why it should not become law. He frequently cited the Virginia Declaration of Rights in support of his arguments. Madison pushed the national conversation further in the direction of individual free exercise of religion and away from community-endorsed religion.

The practical manifestation of Madison's efforts was that the Virginia Assembly in 1785 adopted Thomas Jefferson's Statute of Religious Liberty, originally introduced in 1779. The Virginia Senate passed the statute in January 1786.

SOURCE: *The Essential Bill of Rights*, ed. Gordon Lloyd and Margie Lloyd, (Lanham, MD: University Press of America, 1998), 224–230; https://goo.gl/q7UB62. The Arabic numerals and the footnote references are in the original. Editorial notes and additions to notes are in brackets. We have modernized spelling and capitalization.

To the Honorable the General Assembly of the Commonwealth of Virginia:

We, the subscribers, citizens of the said Commonwealth, having taken into serious consideration a bill printed by order of the last session of General

Assembly, entitled "A Bill establishing a provision for Teachers of the Christian Religion," and conceiving that the same, if finally armed with the sanctions of a law, will be a dangerous abuse of power, are bound as faithful members of a free state to remonstrate against it, and to declare the reasons by which we are determined. We remonstrate against the said bill—

1. Because we hold it for a fundamental and undeniable truth, "that religion, or the duty which we owe to our Creator, and the manner of discharging it, can be directed only by reason and conviction, not by force or violence."[1] The religion, then, of every man must be left to the conviction and conscience of every man; and it is the right of every man to exercise it, as these may dictate. This right is in its nature an unalienable right. It is unalienable, because the opinions of men, depending only on the evidence contemplated by their own minds, cannot follow the dictates of other men. It is unalienable, also, because what is here a right towards men is a duty towards the Creator. It is the duty of every man to render to the Creator such homage, and such only, as he believes to be acceptable to him. This duty is precedent, both in order of time and in degree of obligation, to the claims of civil society. Before any man can be considered as a member of civil society, he must be considered as a subject of the Governor of the Universe, and if a member of civil society who enters into any subordinate association must always do it with a reservation of his duty to the general authority, much more must every man who becomes a member of any particular civil society do it with a saving of his allegiance to the Universal Sovereign. We maintain, therefore, that in matters of religion, no man's right is abridged by the institution of civil society, and that religion is wholly exempt from its cognizance. True it is, that no other rule exists by which any question which may divide a society can be ultimately determined than the will of the majority; but it is also true that the majority may trespass on the rights of the minority.

2. Because, if religion be exempt from the authority of the society at large, still less can it be subject to that of the legislative body. The latter are but the creatures and vicegerents[2] of the former. Their jurisdiction is both derivative and limited. It is limited with regard to the co-ordinate departments; more necessarily is it limited with regard to the constituents. The preservation of a free government requires, not merely that the metes and bounds[3] which separate each department of power be invariably maintained, but more especially

---

[1] Virginia Declaration of Rights, Article 16
[2] A vicegerent is a king-appointed substitute.
[3] Metes and bounds was a system of setting the boundary of a property.

that neither of them be suffered to overleap the great barrier which defends the rights of the people. The rulers who are guilty of such an encroachment exceed the commission from which they derive their authority, and are tyrants. The people who submit to it are governed by laws made neither by themselves nor by an authority derived from them, and are slaves.

3. Because it is proper to take alarm at the first experiment on our liberties. We hold this prudent jealousy to be the first duty of citizens, and one of the noblest characteristics of the late Revolution. The freemen of America did not wait till usurped power had strengthened itself by exercise, and entangled the question in precedents. They saw all the consequences in the principle, and they avoided the consequences by denying the principle. We revere this lesson too much soon to forget it. Who does not see that the same authority which can establish Christianity, in exclusion of all other religions, may establish, with the same ease, any particular sect of Christians, in exclusion of all other sects? That the same authority which can force a citizen to contribute three pence only of his property for the support of any one establishment, may force him to conform to any other establishment in all cases whatsoever?

4. Because the bill violates that equality which ought to be the basis of every law, and which is more indispensible, in proportion as the validity or expediency of any law is more liable to be impeached. "If all men are by nature equally free and independent,"[4] all men are to be considered as entering into society on equal conditions; as relinquishing no more, and therefore retaining no less, one than another, of their natural rights. Above all are they to be considered as retaining an "equal title to the free exercise of religion according to the dictates of conscience."[5] Whilst we assert for ourselves a freedom to embrace, to profess, and to observe, the religion which we believe to be of divine origin, we cannot deny an equal freedom to them whose minds have not yet yielded to the evidence which has convinced us. If this freedom be abused, it is an offence against God, not against man. To God, therefore, not to man, must an account of it be rendered. As the bill violates equality by subjecting some to peculiar burdens, so it violates the same principle by granting to others peculiar exemptions. Are the Quakers and Menonists[6] the only sects who think a compulsive support of their religions unnecessary and unwarrantable? Can their piety alone be entrusted with the care of public worship? Ought their religions to be endowed above all others with

---

[4] Declaration of Rights, Article I
[5] Article 16
[6] Mennonites

extraordinary privileges, by which proselytes may be enticed from all others? We think too favorably of the justice and good sense of these denominations to believe that they either covet pre-eminences over their fellow citizens, or that they will be seduced by them from the common opposition to the measure.

5. Because the bill implies, either that the civil magistrate is a competent judge of religious truths, or that he may employ religion as an engine of civil policy. The first is an arrogant pretension, falsified by the contradictory opinions of rulers in all ages, and throughout the world; the second, an unhallowed perversion of the means of salvation.

6. Because the establishment proposed by the bill is not requisite for the support of the Christian religion. To say that it is, is a contradiction to the Christian religion itself, for every page of it disavows a dependence on the powers of this world. It is a contradiction to fact, for it is known that this religion both existed and flourished, not only without the support of human laws, but in spite of every opposition from them; and not only during the period of miraculous aid, but long after it had been left to its own evidence and the ordinary care of providence. Nay, it is a contradiction in terms; for a religion not invented by human policy must have pre-existed and been supported, before it was established by human policy. It is, moreover, to weaken in those who profess this religion a pious confidence in its innate excellence and the patronage of its Author; and to foster in those who still reject it a suspicion that its friends are too conscious of its fallacies to trust it to its own merits.

7. Because experience witnesseth that ecclesiastical establishments, instead of maintaining the purity and efficacy of religion, have had a contrary operation. During almost fifteen centuries has the legal establishment of Christianity been on trial. What have been its fruits? More or less, in all places, pride and indolence in the clergy; ignorance and servility in the laity; in both, superstition, bigotry, and persecution. Enquire of the teachers of Christianity for the ages in which it appeared in its greatest luster; those of every sect point to the ages prior to its incorporation with civil policy. Propose a restoration of this primitive state, in which its teachers depended on the voluntary rewards of their flocks; many of them predict its downfall. On which side ought their testimony to have greatest weight; when for or when against their interest?

8. Because the establishment in question is not necessary for the support of civil government. If it be urged as necessary for the support of civil government only as it is a means of supporting religion, and it be not necessary

for the latter purpose, it cannot be necessary for the former. If religion be not within the cognizance of civil government, how can its legal establishment be necessary to civil government? What influence, in fact, have ecclesiastical establishments had on civil society? In some instances they have been seen to erect a spiritual tyranny on the ruins of the civil authority; in many instances they have been seen upholding the thrones of political tyranny; in no instance have they been seen the guardians of the liberties of the people. Rulers who wished to subvert the public liberty may have found an established clergy convenient auxiliaries. A just government, instituted to secure and perpetuate it, needs them not. Such a government will be best supported by protecting every citizen in the enjoyment of his religion with the same equal hand which protects his person and his property; by neither invading the equal rights of any sect, nor suffering any sect to invade those of another.

9. Because the proposed establishment is a departure from that generous policy which, offering an asylum to the persecuted and oppressed of every nation and religion, promised a luster to our country, and an accession to the number of its citizens. What a melancholy mark is the bill of sudden degeneracy! Instead of holding forth an asylum to the persecuted, it is itself a signal of persecution. It degrades from the equal rank of citizens all those whose opinions in religion do not bend to those of the legislative authority. Distant as it may be in its present form from the Inquisition, it differs from it only in degree. The one is the first step, the other the last, in the career of intolerance. The magnanimous sufferer under this cruel scourge in foreign regions must view the bill as a beacon on our coast warning him to seek some other haven, where liberty and philanthropy, in their due extent, may offer a more certain repose from his troubles.

10. Because it will have a like tendency to banish our citizens. The allurements presented by other situations are every day thinning their number. To superadd a fresh motive to emigration by revoking the liberty which they now enjoy would be the same species of folly which has dishonored and depopulated flourishing kingdoms.

11. Because it will destroy that moderation and harmony which the forbearance of our laws to intermeddle with religion has produced among its several sects. Torrents of blood have been spilt in the old world by vain attempts of the secular arm to extinguish religious discord by proscribing all difference in religious opinion. Time has at length revealed the true remedy. Every relaxation of narrow and rigorous policy, wherever it has been tried, has been found to assuage the disease. The American theatre has exhibited proofs that equal and complete liberty, if it does not wholly eradicate it,

sufficiently destroys its malignant influence on the health and prosperity of the state. If, with the salutary effects of this system under our own eyes, we begin to contract the bounds of religious freedom, we know no name that will too severely reproach our folly. At least, let warning be taken at the first fruits of the threatened innovation. The very appearance of the bill has transformed "that Christian forbearance, love and charity,"[7] which of late mutually prevailed, into animosities and jealousies, which may not soon be appeased. What mischiefs may not be dreaded, should this enemy to the public quiet be armed with the force of a law?

12. Because the policy of the bill is adverse to the diffusion of the light of Christianity. The first wish of those who enjoy this precious gift ought to be, that it may be imparted to the whole race of mankind. Compare the number of those who have as yet received it with the number still remaining under the dominion of false religions, and how small is the former! Does the policy of the bill tend to lessen the disproportion? No; it at once discourages those who are strangers to the light of revelation from coming into the region of it, and countenances by example the nations who continue in darkness in shutting out those who might convey it to them. Instead of leveling as far as possible, every obstacle to the victorious progress of truth, the bill, with an ignoble and unchristian timidity, would circumscribe it with a wall of defense against the encroachments of error.

13. Because attempts to enforce, by legal sanctions, acts obnoxious to so great a proportion of citizens, tend to enervate the laws in general, and to slacken the bands of society. If it be difficult to execute any law which is not generally deemed necessary or salutary, what must be the case where it is deemed invalid and dangerous? And what may be the effect of so striking an example of impotency in the government on its general authority?

14. Because a measure of such singular magnitude and delicacy ought not to be imposed without the clearest evidence that it is called for by a majority of citizens; and no satisfactory method is yet proposed by which the voice of the majority in this case may be determined, or its influence secured. "The people of the respective counties are, indeed, requested to signify their opinion respecting the adoption of the bill to the next session of assembly." But the representation must be made equal before the voice either of the Representatives or of the counties will be that of the people. Our hope is, that neither of the former will, after due consideration, espouse the dangerous principle of

---

[7] Declaration of Rights, Article 16

the bill. Should the event disappoint us, it will still leave us in full confidence that a fair appeal to the latter will reverse the sentence against our liberties.

15. Because, finally, "the equal right of every citizen to the free exercise of his religion, according to the dictates of conscience," is held by the same tenure with all our other rights. If we recur to its origin, it is equally the gift of nature; if we weigh its importance, it cannot be less dear to us; if we consult the declaration of those rights "which pertain to the good people of Virginia as the basis and foundation of government,"[8] it is enumerated with equal solemnity, or rather studied emphasis. Either, then, we must say, that the will of the legislature is the only measure of their authority, and that in the plenitude of that authority they may sweep away all our fundamental rights, or, that they are bound to leave this particular right untouched and sacred. Either we must say, that they may control the freedom of the press, may abolish the trial by jury, may swallow up the executive and judiciary powers of the state; nay, that they may despoil us of our very right of suffrage, and erect themselves into an independent and hereditary assembly; or we must say, that they have no authority to enact into law the bill under consideration.

We, the subscribers, say that the General Assembly of this commonwealth have no such authority: And in order that no effort may be omitted on our part against so dangerous an usurpation, we oppose to it this remonstrance; earnestly praying, as we are in duty bound, that the Supreme Lawgiver of the universe, by illuminating those to whom it is addressed, may, on the one hand, turn their councils from every act which would affront his holy prerogative, or violate the trust committed to them; and on the other, guide them into every measure which may be worthy of his blessing, redound to their own praise, and establish more firmly the liberties, the prosperity, and the happiness of the commonwealth.

---

[8] Declaration of Rights, title

The Northwest Ordinance

July 13, 1787

T here are six important reasons to reflect on how the Northwest Ordinance is important to the emergence of the Bill of Rights. First, the ordinance moved the conversation over rights from the colonial and state level to the national level. Second, given the expectation that people would inhabit these territories, the ordinance addressed the questions: Do people travel with their rights from their former domicile, and would there be rights "waiting" for them when they arrive? Third, Section 2 of the Northwest Ordinance represented the first federal measure abolishing the traditional laws of primogeniture governing the distribution of property. Primogeniture had meant that the first-born son inherited all of his father's property. In England, this rule helped sustain a landed aristocracy. In the several states, primogeniture was abolished in the years following independence. Fourth, the six articles of the ordinance outlined the mutual obligations between the existing states and the new states to be created on an equal footing with them, from within the territory. Fifth, in these new states, republican governmenst would be based on the principles of religious liberty. And finally, according to Article 6, there would be neither slavery nor involuntary servitude in the territory.

SOURCE: *Documents Illustrative of the Formation of the Union of the American States*, Selected, Arranged and Indexed by Charles C. Tansill (Washington, DC: Government Printing Office, 1927), 47–54. See also *The Essential Bill of Rights*, ed. Gordon Lloyd and Margie Lloyd, (Lanham, MD: University Press of America, 1998), 253–256.

An Ordinance for the Government of the Territory of the United States Northwest of the River Ohio.

Section 1. Be it ordained by the United States in Congress assembled, that the said territory, for the purposes of temporary government, be one district, subject, however, to be divided into two districts, as future circumstances may, in the opinion of Congress, make it expedient.

Sec 2. Be it ordained by the authority aforesaid, that the estates, both of resident and nonresident proprietors in the said territory, dying intestate, shall descend to, and be distributed among their children, and the descendants of a deceased child, in equal parts; the descendants of a deceased child or grandchild to take the share of their deceased parent in equal parts among them: And where there shall be no children or descendants, then in equal parts to the next of kin in equal degree; and among collaterals, the children of a deceased brother or sister of the intestate shall have, in equal parts among them, their deceased parents' share; and there shall in no case be a distinction between kindred of the whole and half blood; saving, in all cases, to the widow of the intestate her third part of the real estate for life, and one third part of the personal estate; and this law relative to descents and dower, shall remain in full force until altered by the legislature of the district. And until the Governor and judges shall adopt laws as hereinafter mentioned, estates in the said territory may be devised or bequeathed by wills in writing, signed and sealed by him or her in whom the estate may be (being of full age), and attested by three witnesses; and real estates may be conveyed by lease and release, or bargain and sale, signed, sealed and delivered by the person being of full age, in whom the estate may be, and attested by two witnesses, provided such wills be duly proved, and such conveyances be acknowledged, or the execution thereof duly proved, and be recorded within one year after proper magistrates, courts, and registers shall be appointed for that purpose; and personal property may be transferred by delivery; saving, however to the French and Canadian inhabitants, and other settlers of the Kaskaskies, St. Vincents[1] and the neighboring villages who have heretofore professed themselves citizens of Virginia, their laws and customs now in force among them, relative to the descent and conveyance, of property.

Sec. 3. Be it ordained by the authority aforesaid, that there shall be appointed from time to time by Congress, a Governor, whose commission shall continue in force for the term of three years, unless sooner revoked by Congress; he shall reside in the district, and have a freehold[2] estate therein in 1,000 acres of land, while in the exercise of his office.

Sec. 4. There shall be appointed from time to time by Congress, a secretary, whose commission shall continue in force for four years unless sooner revoked; he shall reside in the district, and have a freehold estate therein in 500 acres of land, while in the exercise of his office. It shall be his duty to

---

[1] French settlements established earlier in 18th century, now part of the northwest territory of the United States
[2] "Freehold" means property held entirely by the owner, without obligation to anyone else.

keep and preserve the acts and laws passed by the legislature, and the public records of the district, and the proceedings of the Governor in his executive department, and transmit authentic copies of such acts and proceedings, every six months, to the secretary of Congress: There shall also be appointed a court to consist of three judges, any two of whom to form a court, who shall have a common law jurisdiction, and reside in the district, and have each therein a freehold estate in 500 acres of land while in the exercise of their offices; and their commissions shall continue in force during good behavior.

Sec. 5. The Governor and judges, or a majority of them, shall adopt and publish in the district such laws of the original states, criminal and civil, as may be necessary and best suited to the circumstances of the district, and report them to Congress from time to time: which laws shall be in force in the district until the organization of the General Assembly therein, unless disapproved of by Congress; but afterwards the Legislature shall have authority to alter them as they shall think fit.

Sec. 6. The Governor, for the time being, shall be commander in chief of the militia, appoint and commission all officers in the same below the rank of general officers; all general officers shall be appointed and commissioned by Congress.

Sec. 7. Previous to the organization of the General Assembly, the Governor shall appoint such magistrates and other civil officers in each county or township, as he shall find necessary for the preservation of the peace and good order in the same: After the General Assembly shall be organized, the powers and duties of the magistrates and other civil officers shall be regulated and defined by the said assembly; but all magistrates and other civil officers not herein otherwise directed, shall during the continuance of this temporary government, be appointed by the Governor.

Sec. 8. For the prevention of crimes and injuries, the laws to be adopted or made shall have force in all parts of the district, and for the execution of process, criminal and civil, the Governor shall make proper divisions thereof; and he shall proceed from time to time as circumstances may require, to lay out the parts of the district in which the Indian titles shall have been extinguished, into counties and townships, subject, however, to such alterations as may thereafter be made by the legislature.

Sec. 9. So soon as there shall be five thousand free male inhabitants of full age in the district, upon giving proof thereof to the Governor, they shall receive authority, with time and place, to elect a representative from their counties or townships to represent them in the General Assembly: Provided, that, for every five hundred free male inhabitants, there shall be one representative, and so on progressively with the number of free male inhabitants shall the right of representation increase, until the number of representatives shall amount to twenty-five; after which, the number and proportion of representatives shall be regulated by the legislature: Provided, that no person be eligible or qualified to act as a representative unless he shall have been a citizen of one of the United States three years, and be a resident in the district, or unless he shall have resided in the district three years; and, in either case, shall likewise hold in his own right, in fee simple,[3] two hundred acres of land within the same; Provided, also, that a freehold in fifty acres of land in the district, having been a citizen of one of the states, and being resident in the district, or the like freehold and two years residence in the district, shall be necessary to qualify a man as an elector of a representative.

Sec. 10. The representatives thus elected, shall serve for the term of two years; and, in case of the death of a representative, or removal from office, the Governor shall issue a writ to the county or township for which he was a member, to elect another in his stead, to serve for the residue of the term.

Sec. 11. The General Assembly or legislature shall consist of the Governor, Legislative Council , and a House of Representatives. The Legislative Council shall consist of five members, to continue in office five years, unless sooner removed by Congress; any three of whom to be a quorum: and the members of the council shall be nominated and appointed in the following manner, to wit: As soon as representatives shall be elected, the Governor shall appoint a time and place for them to meet together; and, when met, they shall nominate ten persons, residents in the district, and each possessed of a freehold in five hundred acres of land, and return their names to Congress; five of whom Congress shall appoint and commission to serve as aforesaid; and, whenever a vacancy shall happen in the council, by death or removal from office, the house of representatives shall nominate two persons, qualified as aforesaid, for each vacancy, and return their names to Congress; one of whom congress shall appoint and commission for the residue of the term. And every five years, four months at least before the expiration of the time of service of the members of council, the said house shall nominate ten persons, qualified as aforesaid, and return their names to Congress; five of whom Congress shall appoint and commission to serve as members of the

---

[3] "Fee simple" means holding land without obligation to anyone else. It is a synonym for "freehold."

council five years, unless sooner removed. And the Governor, legislative council, and house of representatives, shall have authority to make laws in all cases, for the good government of the district, not repugnant to the principles and articles in this ordinance established and declared. And all bills, having passed by a majority in the house, and by a majority in the council, shall be referred to the Governor for his assent; but no bill, or legislative act whatever, shall be of any force without his assent. The Governor shall have power to convene, prorogue, and dissolve the General Assembly, when, in his opinion, it shall be expedient.

Sec. 12. The Governor, judges, legislative council, secretary, and such other officers as Congress shall appoint in the district, shall take an oath or affirmation of fidelity and of office; the Governor before the president of congress, and all other officers before the Governor. As soon as a legislature shall be formed in the district, the council and house assembled in one room, shall have authority, by joint ballot, to elect a delegate to Congress, who shall have a seat in Congress, with a right of debating but not voting during this temporary government.

Sec. 13. And, for extending the fundamental principles of civil and religious liberty, which form the basis whereon these republics, their laws and constitutions are erected; to fix and establish those principles as the basis of all laws, constitutions, and governments, which forever hereafter shall be formed in the said territory: to provide also for the establishment of states, and permanent government therein, and for their admission to a share in the federal councils on an equal footing with the original States, at as early periods as may be consistent with the general interest:

Sec. 14. It is hereby ordained and declared by the authority aforesaid, That the following articles shall be considered as articles of compact between the original States and the people and States in the said territory and forever remain unalterable, unless by common consent, to wit:

Art. 1. No person, demeaning himself in a peaceable and orderly manner, shall ever be molested on account of his mode of worship or religious sentiments, in the said territory.

Art. 2. The inhabitants of the said territory shall always be entitled to the benefits of the writ of habeas corpus,[4] and of the trial by jury; of a proportionate representation of the people in the legislature; and of judicial proceedings according to the course of the common law. All persons shall

---

[4] A written order from a court that a person be brought before it, issued in order to free someone being held unless legal grounds are offered for his detention.

be bailable,[5] unless for capital offenses, where the proof shall be evident or the presumption great. All fines shall be moderate; and no cruel or unusual punishments shall be inflicted. No man shall be deprived of his liberty or property, but by the judgment of his peers or the law of the land; and, should the public exigencies make it necessary, for the common preservation, to take any person's property, or to demand his particular services, full compensation shall be made for the same. And, in the just preservation of rights and property, it is understood and declared, that no law ought ever to be made, or have force in the said territory, that shall, in any manner whatever, interfere with or affect private contracts or engagements, bona fide, and without fraud, previously formed.

Art. 3. Religion, morality, and knowledge, being necessary to good government and the happiness of mankind, schools and the means of education shall forever be encouraged. The utmost good faith shall always be observed towards the Indians; their lands and property shall never be taken from them without their consent; and, in their property, rights, and liberty, they shall never be invaded or disturbed, unless in just and lawful wars authorized by Congress; but laws founded in justice and humanity, shall from time to time be made for preventing wrongs being done to them, and for preserving peace and friendship with them.

Art. 4. The said territory, and the states which may be formed therein, shall forever remain a part of this Confederacy of the United States of America, subject to the Articles of Confederation, and to such alterations therein as shall be constitutionally made; and to all the acts and ordinances of the United States in Congress assembled, conformable thereto. The inhabitants and settlers in the said territory shall be subject to pay a part of the federal debts contracted or to be contracted, and a proportional part of the expenses of government, to be apportioned on them by Congress according to the same common rule and measure by which apportionments thereof shall be made on the other states; and the taxes for paying their proportion shall be laid and levied by the authority and direction of the legislatures of the district or districts, or new states, as in the original states, within the time agreed upon by the United States in Congress assembled. The legislatures of those districts or new states, shall never interfere with the primary disposal of the soil by the United States in Congress assembled, nor with any regulations Congress may find necessary for securing the title in such soil to the bona

---

[5] Eligible, while awaiting trial, for release, offered on the basis of a monetary bond forfeited if the person fails to appear for trial.

fide purchasers. No tax shall be imposed on lands the property of the United States; and, in no case, shall nonresident proprietors be taxed higher than residents. The navigable waters leading into the Mississippi and St. Lawrence, and the carrying places between the same, shall be common highways and forever free, as well to the inhabitants of the said territory as to the citizens of the United States, and those of any other states that may be admitted into the confederacy, without any tax, impost, or duty therefor.

Art. 5. There shall be formed in the said territory, not less than three nor more than five states; and the boundaries of the states, as soon as Virginia shall alter her act of cession,[6] and consent to the same, shall become fixed and established as follows. . . . And, whenever any of the said states shall have sixty thousand free inhabitants therein, such state shall be admitted, by its delegates, into the Congress of the United States, on an equal footing with the original states in all respects whatever, and shall be at liberty to form a permanent constitution and State government: Provided, the constitution and government so to be formed, shall be republican, and in conformity to the principles contained in these articles; and, so far as it can be consistent with the general interest of the confederacy, such admission shall be allowed at an earlier period, and when there may be a less number of free inhabitants in the state than sixty thousand.

Art. 6. There shall be neither slavery nor involuntary servitude in the said territory, otherwise than in the punishment of crimes whereof the party shall have been duly convicted: Provided, always, that any person escaping into the same, from whom labor or service is lawfully claimed in any one of the original states, such fugitive may be lawfully reclaimed and conveyed to the person claiming his or her labor or service as aforesaid.

Be it ordained by the authority aforesaid, that the resolutions of the 23rd of April, 1784,[7] relative to the subject of this ordinance, be, and the same are hereby repealed and declared null and void.

Done by the United States, in Congress assembled, the 13th day of July, in the year of our Lord 1787, and of their sovereignty and independence the twelfth.

---

[6] By its original charter, Virginia, like several other states, had claims on western lands. In most cases, the states ceded these claims to the federal government during the 1780s.

[7] An earlier ordinance passed by the Confederation Congress dealing with the Northwest Territory

Objections at the Constitutional Convention

September 10, 12, 15, and 17, 1787

Edmund Randolph (Virginia), George Mason (Virginia) and Elbridge Gerry (Massachusetts) were at the Constitutional Convention from the beginning and stayed to the very end. During their eighty-eight days at the Convention, their views went through some dramatic changes. They supported the initial Virginia plan, which Randolph proposed early in the Convention, in May 1787. Among other things, this plan called for a bicameral national legislature with seats apportioned by population. States with smaller populations disliked this way of apportioning seats, leading to the proposal that in the lower house (the Senate), states receive equal representation.

By the end of the Convention, however, Randolph, Mason, and Gerry declined to support the Constitution. Is it possible to locate the moment or issue when they started to have reservations about the direction of the conversation? Randolph was the first to state his objections. He did so on September 10. Mason and Gerry's call for a bill of rights was rejected on September 12. Randolph elaborated his concerns on September 15. He was joined on that day by Mason and then by Gerry. Mason also wrote his objections on his copy of the Committee of Style Report. Their decision to withhold their signatures became important in the debate over the ratification of the Constitution.

These excerpts of the debates in the Convention show that the call for a bill of rights was one aspect of a larger concern about the power of the proposed national government in relation to the rights of the states and the people. One of the mysteries is why the delegates, many of whom were involved with writing a bill of rights for their own state constitutions—especially Madison—dismissed a request that a bill of rights be incorporated within the proposed Constitution. One answer is that in September 1787, Madison and others were more interested in establishing the Constitution than constraining it in the direction of the Articles of Confederation.

SOURCE: Gordon Lloyd, ed., *Debates in the Federal Convention of 1787 by James Madison, a Member* (Ashland, OH: Ashbrook Center, 2014), 508–11, 544–46; "George Mason's Objections to the Constitution," George Mason Manuscript Collection, Gunston Hall Library and Archives, https://goo.gl/Dwb5wL. We have numbered within brackets Mason's ten objections.

September 10

Mr. GERRY moved to reconsider Articles 21 and 22; from the latter of which "for the approbation of Congress," had been struck out.[1] He objected to proceeding to change the government without the approbation of Congress, as being improper, and giving just umbrage to that body. He repeated his objections, also, to an annulment of the Confederation with so little scruple or formality.

Mr. HAMILTON[2] concurred with Mr. GERRY as to the indecorum of not requiring the approbation of Congress. He considered this as a necessary ingredient in the transaction. He thought it wrong, also, to allow nine states, as provided by Article 21, to institute a new government on the ruins of the existing one. He would propose, as a better modification of the two articles (21 and 22), that the plan should be sent to Congress, in order that the same, if approved by them, may be communicated to the state legislatures, to the end that they may refer it to state conventions; each legislature declaring, that, if the convention of the state should think the plan ought to take effect among nine ratifying states, the same should take effect accordingly.

Mr. GORHAM.[3] Some states will say that nine states shall be sufficient to establish the plan; others will require unanimity for the purpose, and the different and conditional ratifications will defeat the plan altogether.

Mr. HAMILTON. No convention convinced of the necessity of the plan will refuse to give it effect, on the adoption by nine states. He thought this mode less exceptionable than the one proposed in the article: while it would attain the same end.

Mr. FITZSIMONS[4] remarked, that the words, "for their approbation," had been struck out in order to save Congress from the necessity of an act inconsistent with the Articles of Confederation under which they held their authority.

Mr. RANDOLPH declared if no change should be made in this part of the

---

[1] For these articles in the draft of the Constitution, see the Committee of Detail Report, Document 12 of *The American Founding: Core Documents*, edited Gordon Lloyd (Ashbrook Press, 2017), 97.
[2] Alexander Hamilton, New York
[3] Nathaniel Gorham, Massachusetts
[4] Thomas Fitzsimons, Pennsylvania

plan, he should be obliged to dissent from the whole of it. He had from the beginning, he said, been convinced that radical changes in the system of the Union were necessary. Under this conviction he had brought forward a set of republican propositions, as the basis and outline of a reform. These republican propositions had, however, much to his regret, been widely, and, in his opinion, irreconcilably departed from. In this state of things, it was his idea, and he accordingly meant to propose, that the state conventions should be at liberty to offer amendments to the plan; and that these should be submitted to a second general convention, with full power to settle the Constitution finally. He did not expect to succeed in this proposition, but the discharge of his duty in making the attempt would give quiet to his own mind.

Mr. WILSON[5] was against a reconsideration for any of the purposes which had been mentioned.

Mr. KING[6] thought it would be more respectful to Congress, to submit the plan generally to them than in such a form as expressly and necessarily to require their approbation or disapprobation. The assent of nine states he considered as sufficient; and that it was more proper to make this a part of the Constitution itself, than to provide for it by a supplemental or distinct recommendation.

Mr. GERRY urged the indecency and pernicious tendency of dissolving, in so slight a manner, the solemn obligations of the Articles of Confederation. If nine out of thirteen can dissolve the compact, six out of nine will be just as able to dissolve the new one hereafter.

Mr. SHERMAN[7] was in favor of Mr. KING'S idea of submitting the plan generally to Congress. He thought nine states ought to be made sufficient; but that it would be better to make it a separate act, and in some such form as that intimated by Col. HAMILTON, than to make it a particular article of the Constitution.

On the question for reconsidering the two articles, 21 and 22,— Connecticut, New Jersey, Delaware, Maryland, Virginia, North Carolina, Georgia, aye,—7; Massachusetts, Pennsylvania, South Carolina, no,—3; New Hampshire, divided.

... Mr. RANDOLPH took this opportunity to state his objections to the system. They turned on the Senate's being made the court of impeachment for

---

[5] James Wilson, Pennsylvania
[6] Rufus King, Massachusetts
[7] Roger Sherman, Connecticut

trying the Executive,—on the necessity of three-fourths instead of two-thirds of each House to overrule the negative of the President,—on the smallness of the number of the Representative branch,—on the want of limitation to a standing army,—on the general clause concerning necessary and proper laws,—on the want of some particular restraint on navigation acts,—on the power to lay duties on exports,—on the authority of the general legislature to interpose on the application of the Executives of the states,—on the want of a more definite boundary between the general and state legislatures,—and between the general and state judiciaries,—on the unqualified power of the President to pardon treasons,—on the want of some limit to the power of the legislature in regulating their own compensations. With these difficulties in his mind, what course, he asked, was he to pursue? Was he to promote the establishment of a plan which he verily believed would end in tyranny? He was unwilling, he said, to impede the wishes and judgment of the Convention, but he must keep himself free, in case he should be honored with a seat in the convention of his state, to act according to the dictates of his judgment. The only mode in which his embarrassment could be removed was that of submitting the plan to Congress, to go from them to the state legislatures, and from these to state conventions, having power to adopt, reject, or amend; the process to close with another general convention, with full power to adopt or reject the alterations proposed by the state conventions, and to establish finally the government. He accordingly proposed a resolution to this effect.

Doctor FRANKLIN[8] seconded the motion.

Colonel MASON urged and obtained that the motion should lie on the table for a day or two, to see what steps might be taken with regard to the parts of the system objected to by Mr. RANDOLPH.

Mr. PINCKNEY moved, "that it be an instruction to the committee for revising the style and arrangement of the articles agreed on, to prepare an address to the people, to accompany the present Constitution, and to be laid, with the same, before the United States in Congress."

The motion itself was referred to the committee, *nem. con.*[9]

Mr. RANDOLPH moved to refer to the committee, also, a motion relating to pardons in cases of treason; which was agreed to, *nem. con.*

Adjourned.

---

[8] Benjamin Franklin, Pennsylvania

[9] an abbreviation of nemine contradicente, Latin for "no one dissenting"

September 12

Colonel MASON ... wished the plan had been prefaced with a bill of rights, and would second a motion if made for the purpose. It would give great quiet to the people; and with the aid of the state declarations, a bill might be prepared in a few hours.

Mr. GERRY concurred in the idea and moved for a committee to prepare a bill of rights.

Colonel MASON seconded the motion.

Mr. SHERMAN, was for securing the rights of the people where requisite. The state declaration of rights are not repealed by this Constitution; and being in force are sufficient. There are many cases where juries are proper which cannot be discriminated. The legislature may be safely trusted.

Colonel MASON. The laws of the U.S. are to be paramount to state bills of rights.

On the question for a committee to prepare a bill of rights,—N.H. no. Mas. absent. Ct. no. N.J. no. Pa. no. Del. no. Md. no. Va. no. N.C. no. S.C. no. Geo. no.

September 15

Mr. RANDOLPH animadverting[10] on the indefinite and dangerous power given by the Constitution to Congress, expressing the pain he felt at differing from the body of the Convention on the close of the great and awful subject of their labors, and anxiously wishing for some accommodating expedient which would relieve him from his embarrassments, made a motion importing, "that amendments to the plan might be offered by the state conventions, which should be submitted to, and finally decided on by, another general convention." Should this proposition be disregarded, it would, he said, be impossible for him to put his name to the instrument. Whether he should oppose it afterwards, he would not then decide; but he would not deprive himself of the freedom to do so in his own state, if that course should be prescribed by his final judgment.

Colonel MASON seconded and followed Mr. RANDOLPH in animadversions on the dangerous power and structure of the government, concluding that it would end either in monarchy, or a tyrannical aristocracy; which,

---

[10] pointing critically to

he was in doubt, but one or other, he was sure. This Constitution had been formed without the knowledge or idea of the people. A second convention will know more of the sense of the people, and be able to provide a system more consonant to it. It was improper to say to the people, take this or nothing. As the Constitution now stands, he could neither give it his support or vote in Virginia; and he could not sign here what he could not support there. With the expedient of another convention, as proposed, he could sign.

Mr. PINCKNEY.[11] These declarations from members so respectable, at the close of this important scene, give a peculiar solemnity to the present moment. He descanted[12] on the consequences of calling forth the deliberations and amendments of the different states, on the subject of government at large. Nothing but confusion and contrariety will spring from the experiment. The states will never agree in their plans, and the deputies to a second convention, coming together under the discordant impressions of their constituents, will never agree. Conventions are serious things, and ought not to be repeated. He was not without objections, as well as others, to the plan. He objected to the contemptible weakness and dependence of the Executive. He objected to the power of a majority, only, of Congress, over commerce. But apprehending the danger of a general confusion, and an ultimate decision by the sword, he should give the plan his support.

Mr. GERRY stated the objections which determined him to withhold his name from the Constitution:

1. the duration and re-eligibility of the Senate; 2. the power of the House of Representatives to conceal its journals; 3. the power of Congress over the places of election; 4. the unlimited power of Congress over its own compensation; 5. that Massachusetts has not a due share of representatives allotted to it; 6. that three-fifths of the blacks are to be represented, as if they were freemen; 7. that under the power over commerce, monopolies may be established; 8. the Vice President being made head of the Senate.

He could, however, he said, get over all these, if the rights of the citizens were not rendered insecure,—first, by the general power of the legislature to make what laws they may please to call "necessary and proper"; secondly, to raise armies and money without limit; thirdly, to establish a tribunal without juries, which will be a Star Chamber[13] as to civil cases. Under such a view of

---

[11] Charles Pinckney, South Carolina
[12] spoke at length
[13] The Star Chamber existed as an English court of law between the late fifteenth and mid-seventeenth centuries. Designed as a supplement to common law courts that

the Constitution, the best that could be done, he conceived, was to provide for a second general convention.

On the question, on the proposition of Mr. RANDOLPH, all the states answered, no.

On the question to agree to the Constitution, as amended, all the states, aye. The Constitution was then ordered to be engrossed, and the House adjourned.

Mason's Objections to the Constitution, September 17, 1787

[1] There is no declaration of rights: and the laws of the general government being paramount to the laws and constitutions of the several states, the declarations of rights, in the separate states, are no security. Nor are the people secured even in the enjoyment of the benefit of the common law, which stands here upon no other foundation than its having been adopted by the respective acts forming the constitutions of the several states.

[2] In the House of Representatives there is not the substance, but the shadow only of representation; which can never produce proper information in the legislature, or inspire confidence in the people.—The laws will, therefore, be generally made by men little concerned in, and unacquainted with, their effects and consequences.

[3] The Senate have the power of altering all money-bills, and of originating appropriations of money, and the salaries of the officers of their own appointment, in conjunction with the President of the United States— although they are not the representatives of the people, or amenable to them. These, with their other great powers (*viz.*[14] their powers in the appointment of ambassadors, and all public officers, in making treaties, and in trying all impeachments), their influence upon, and connection with, the supreme executive from these causes, their duration of office, and their being a constant existing body, almost continually sitting, joined with their being one complete branch of the legislature, will destroy any balance in the government, and enable them to accomplish what usurpations they please upon the rights and liberties of the people.

[4] The judiciary of the United States is so constructed and extended, as

---

would ensure speedier trial and stricter judgments against prominent people, it dispensed with indictments and substituted appointive judges for a jury of commoners. It came to be seen as a tool by which the monarch could enforce his arbitrary will.
[14] abbreviation of the Latin *videlicet*, "namely"

to absorb and destroy the judiciaries of the several states; thereby rendering laws as tedious, intricate, and expensive, and justice as unattainable by a great part of the community, as in England; and enabling the rich to oppress and ruin the poor.

[5] The President of the United States has no constitutional council (a thing unknown in any safe and regular government). He will therefore be unsupported by proper information and advice; and will generally be directed by minions and favorites—or he will become a tool to the Senate—or a council of state will grow out of the principal officers of the great departments—the worst and most dangerous of all ingredients for such a council, in a free country; for they may be induced to join in any dangerous or oppressive measures, to shelter themselves, and prevent an inquiry into their own misconduct in office. Whereas, had a constitutional council been formed (as was proposed) of six members, *viz.*, two from the eastern, two from the middle, and two from the southern states, to be appointed by vote of the states in the House of Representatives, with the same duration and rotation of office as the Senate, the executive would always have had safe and proper information and advice; the President of such a council might have acted as Vice President of the United States, *pro tempore*, upon any vacancy or disability of the chief magistrate, and long continued sessions of the Senate, would in a great measure have been prevented. From this fatal defect of a constitutional council, has arisen the improper power of the Senate, in the appointment of the public officers, and the alarming dependence and connection between that branch of the legislature and the supreme executive. Hence, also, sprung that unnecessary officer, the Vice President, who, for want of other employment, is made President of the Senate, thereby dangerously blending the executive and legislative powers; besides always giving to some one of the states an unnecessary and unjust pre-eminence over the others.

[6] The President of the United States has the unrestrained power of granting pardon for treason; which may be sometimes exercised to screen from punishment those whom he had secretly instigated to commit the crime, and thereby prevent a discovery of his own guilt. By declaring all treaties supreme laws of the land, the executive and the Senate have, in many cases, an exclusive power of legislation, which might have been avoided, by proper distinctions with respect to treaties, and requiring the assent of the House of Representatives, where it could be done with safety.

[7] By requiring only a majority to make all commercial and navigation laws, the five southern states (whose produce and circumstances are totally different from those of the eight northern and eastern states) will be ruined:

for such rigid and premature regulations may be made, as will enable the merchants of the northern and eastern states not only to demand an exorbitant freight, but to monopolize the purchase of the commodities, at their own price, for many years, to the great injury of the landed interest, and the impoverishment of the people: and the danger is the greater, as the gain on one side will be in proportion to the loss on the other. Whereas, requiring two-thirds of the members present in both houses, would have produced mutual moderation, promoted the general interest, and removed an insuperable objection to the adoption of the government.

[8] Under their own construction of the general clause at the end of the enumerated powers, the Congress may grant monopolies in trade and commerce, constitute new crimes, inflict unusual and severe punishments, and extend their power as far as they shall think proper; so that the state legislatures have no security for the powers now presumed to remain to them, or the people for their rights. There is no declaration of any kind for preserving the liberty of the press, the trial by jury in civil cases, nor against the danger of standing armies in time of peace.

[9] The state legislatures are restrained from laying export duties on their own produce—the general legislature is restrained from prohibiting the further importation of slaves for twenty odd years, though such importations render the United States weaker, more vulnerable, and less capable of defense. Both the general legislature, and the state legislatures are expressly prohibited making *ex post facto* laws, though there never was, nor can be, a legislature but must and will make such laws, when necessity and the public safety require them, which will hereafter be a breach of all the constitutions in the union, and afford precedents for other innovations.

[10] This government will commence in a moderate aristocracy; it is at present impossible to foresee whether it will, in its operation, produce a monarchy, or a corrupt oppressive aristocracy; it will most probably vibrate some years between the two, and then terminate in the one or the other.

James Wilson's State House Speech

October 6, 1787

O n September 29, 1787, the Pennsylvania Assembly approved calling elections to select sixty-nine delegates on November 6 to meet in Philadelphia
on November 20 to approve or reject the proposed Constitution. Edmund Randolph (Virginia), George Mason (Virginia) and Elbridge Gerry (Massachusetts)
launched the opposition position with their refusal to sign the Constitution on
September 17 (Document 9). The the ratification campaign began in earnest with
this speech by James Wilson defending the Constitution and the absence of a bill
of rights.

Wilson (1742–1798), born in Scotland, immigrated to the United States when
a young man, and became a leading lawyer and political figure in Pennsylvania.
He signed both the Declaration of Independence and the Constitution. His "State
House" speech, delivered at the State House in Philadelphia, was the first official
defense of the Constitution and responded directly to the objections George Mason
had expressed during the last month of the Convention. It was published in the
Pennsylvania Herald and widely distributed as "an authoritative explanation"
of the Constitution.

Wilson argued that at the state level, a bill of rights is necessary and salutary
because every power "which is not reserved" to the people "is given" to government; but a bill of rights is "superfluous and absurd" at the federal level because
"everything which is not given, is reserved." Both supporters and opponents in the
ratification debates invoked Wilson's theory of "distinction".

Randolph repeated Wilson's argument at the Virginia Ratifying Convention
in June 1788 (Document 17). On August 12, 1788 Hamilton made it in Federalist
84 (Document 19), the last essay published in The New York Packet but the first
in The Federalist to deal directly with the bill of rights controversy. This speech at
the beginning of the ratification campaign became a defining one over the need
for a bill of rights.

SOURCE: We have used the version of the speech prepared by the Liberty Fund; James Wilson, *Collected Works of James Wilson*, edited by Kermit L. Hall and Mark David Hall, (Indianapolis: Liberty Fund, 2007), https://goo.gl/Ztymo5.

Mr. Chairman and Fellow Citizens,

Having received the honor of an appointment to represent you in the late convention, it is perhaps, my duty to comply with the request of many gentlemen whose characters and judgments I sincerely respect, and who have urged, that this would be a proper occasion to lay before you any information, which will serve to explain and elucidate the principles and arrangements of the Constitution that has been submitted to the consideration of the United States. I confess that I am unprepared for so extensive and so important a disquisition; but the insidious attempts which are clandestinely and industriously made to pervert and destroy the new plan, induce me the more readily to engage in its defense; and the impressions of four months constant attention to the subject, have not been so easily effaced as to leave me without an answer to the objections which have been raised.

It will be proper, however, before I enter into the refutation of the charges that are alleged, to mark the leading discrimination between the state constitutions, and the Constitution of the United States. When the people established the powers of legislation under their separate governments, they invested their representatives with every right and authority which they did not in explicit terms reserve; and therefore upon every question, respecting the jurisdiction of the house of assembly, if the frame of government is silent, the jurisdiction is efficient and complete. But in delegating federal powers, another criterion was necessarily introduced, and the congressional authority is to be collected, not from tacit implication, but from the positive grant expressed in the instrument of union. Hence it is evident, that in the former case every thing which is not reserved is given, but in the latter the reverse of the proposition prevails, and every thing which is not given, is reserved. This distinction being recognized, will furnish an answer to those who think the omission of a bill of rights, a defect in the proposed Constitution: for it would have been superfluous and absurd to have stipulated with a federal body of our own creation, that we should enjoy those privileges, of which we are not divested either by the intention or the act, that has brought that body into existence. For instance, the liberty of the press, which has been a copious source of declamation and opposition, what control can proceed from the federal government to shackle or destroy that sacred palladium of national freedom? If indeed, a power similar to that which has been granted for the regulation of commerce, had been granted to regulate literary publications, it would have been as necessary to stipulate that the liberty of the press should be preserved inviolate, as that the impost should be general in its operation. With respect likewise to the particular district of ten miles, which is to be made the seat of federal government, it will undoubtedly be proper to observe this salutary precaution, as there the legislative power will be exclusively lodged in the president, Senate, and House of Representatives of the United States. But this could not be an object with the Convention, for it must naturally depend upon a future compact, to which the citizens immediately interested, will, and ought to be parties; and there is no reason to suspect that so popular a privilege will in that case be neglected. In truth, then, the proposed system possesses no influence whatever upon the press, and it would have been merely nugatory to have introduced a formal declaration upon the subject—nay, that very declaration might have been construed to imply that some degree of power was given, since we undertook to define its extent.

Another objection that has been fabricated against the new Constitution, is expressed in this disingenuous form—"the trial by jury is abolished in civil cases." I must be excused, my fellow citizens, if upon this point, I take advantage of my professional experience to detect the futility of the assertion. Let it be remembered then, that the business of the federal Convention was not local, but general; not limited to the views and establishments of a single state, but co-extensive with the continent, and comprehending the views and establishments of thirteen independent sovereignties. When therefore, this subject was in discussion, we were involved in difficulties which pressed on all sides, and no precedent could be discovered to direct our course. The cases open to a trial by jury differed in the different states, it was therefore impracticable on that ground to have made a general rule. The want of uniformity would have rendered any reference to the practice of the states idle and useless; and it could not, with any propriety, be said that "the trial by jury shall be as heretofore," since there has never existed any federal system of jurisprudence to which the declaration could relate. Besides, it is not in all cases that the trial by jury is adopted in civil questions, for causes depending in courts of admiralty, such as relate to maritime captures, and such as are agitated in courts of equity, do not require the intervention of that tribunal. How then, was the line of discrimination to be drawn? The convention found the task too difficult for them, and they left the business as it stands, in the fullest confidence that no danger could possibly ensue, since the proceedings of the Supreme Court, are to be regulated by the Congress, which is a faithful representation of the people; and the oppression of government is effectually barred, by declaring that in all criminal cases the trial by jury shall be preserved.

This Constitution, it has been further urged, is of a pernicious tendency, because it tolerates a standing army in the time of peace.—This has always been a topic of popular declamation; and yet, I do not know a nation in the world, which has not found it necessary and useful to maintain the appearance of strength in a season of the most profound tranquility. Nor is it a novelty with us; for under the present articles of confederation, congress certainly possesses this reprobated power, and the exercise of that power is proved at this moment by her cantonments along the banks of the Ohio. But what would be our national situation were it otherwise? Every principle of policy must be subverted, and the government must declare war, before they are prepared to carry it on. Whatever may be the provocation, however important the object in view, and however necessary dispatch and secrecy may be, still the declaration must precede the preparation, and the enemy will be informed of your intention, not only before you are equipped for an attack, but even before you are fortified for a defense. The consequence is too obvious to require any further delineation, and no man, who regards the dignity and safety of his country, can deny the necessity of a military force, under the control and with the restrictions which the new constitution provides.

Perhaps there never was a charge made with less reasons than that which predicts the institution of a baneful aristocracy in the federal senate. This body branches into two characters, the one legislative, and the other executive. In its legislative character it can effect no purpose, without the cooperation of the House of Representatives, and in its executive character, it can accomplish no object, without the concurrence of the president. Thus fettered, I do not know any act which the Senate can of itself perform, and such dependence necessarily precludes every idea of influence and superiority. But I will confess that in the organization of this body, a compromise between contending interests is discernable; and when we reflect how various are the laws, commerce, habits, population, and extent of the confederated states, this evidence of mutual concession and accommodation ought rather to command a generous applause, than to excite jealousy and reproach. For my part, my admiration can only be equaled by my astonishment, in beholding so perfect a system, formed from such heterogeneous materials.

The next accusation I shall consider, is that which represents the federal Constitution as not only calculated, but designedly framed, to reduce the state governments to mere corporations, and eventually to annihilate them. Those who have employed the term corporation upon this occasion are not perhaps aware of its extent. In common parlance, indeed, it is generally applied to petty associations for the ease and convenience of a few individuals; but in its enlarged sense, it will comprehend the government of Pennsylvania, the existing union of the states, and even this projected system is nothing more than a formal act of incorporation. But upon what pretense can it be alleged that it was designed to annihilate the state governments? For, I will undertake to prove that upon their existence, depends the existence of the federal plan. For this purpose, permit me to call your attention to the manner in which the president, Senate, and House of Representatives, are proposed to be appointed. The president is to be chosen by electors, nominated in such manner as the legislature of each state may direct; so that if there is no legislature, there can be no electors, and consequently the office of president cannot be supplied. The Senate is to be composed of two senators from each state, chosen by the legislature; and therefore if there is no legislature, there can be no Senate. The House of Representatives, is to be composed of members chosen every second year by the people of the several states, and the electors in each state shall have the qualifications requisite for electors of the most numerous branch of the state legislature,—unless therefore, there is a state legislature, that qualification cannot be ascertained, and the popular branch of the federal constitution must likewise be extinct. From this view, then it is evidently absurd to suppose, that the annihilation of the separate governments will result from their union; or, that having that intention, the authors of the new system would have bound their connection with such indissoluble ties. Let me here advert to an arrangement highly advantageous, for you will perceive, without prejudice to the powers of the legislature in the election of senators, the people at large will acquire an additional privilege in returning members to the house of representatives—whereas, by the present confederation, it is the legislature alone that appoints the delegates to Congress.

The power of direct taxation[1] has likewise been treated as an improper delegation to the federal government; but when we consider it as the duty of that body to provide for the national safety, to support the dignity of the union, and to discharge the debts contracted upon the collective faith of the states for their common benefit, it must be acknowledged, that those upon whom such important obligations are imposed, ought in justice and in policy to possess every means requisite for a faithful performance of their trust. But why should we be alarmed with visionary evils? I will venture to predict, that the great revenue of the United States must, and always will be

---

[1] A direct tax is a tax levied on a person or on property.

raised by impost,[2] for, being at once less obnoxious, and more productive, the interest of the government will be best promoted by the accommodation of the people. Still however, the objects of direct taxation should be within reach in all cases of emergency; and there is no more reason to apprehend oppression in the mode of collecting a revenue from this resource, than in the form of an impost, which, by universal assent, is left to the authority of the federal government. In either case, the force of civil institutions will be adequate to the purpose; and the dread of military violence, which has been assiduously disseminated, must eventually prove the mere effusion of a wild imagination, or a factious spirit. But the salutary consequences that must flow from thus enabling the government to receive and support the credit of the union, will afford another answer to the objections upon this ground. The state of Pennsylvania particularly, which has encumbered itself with the assumption of a great proportion of the public debt, will derive considerable relief and advantage; for, as it was the imbecility of the present confederation, which gave rise to the funding law, that law must naturally expire, when a competent and energetic federal system shall be substituted—the state will then be discharged from an extraordinary burden, and the national creditor will find it to be his interest to return to his original security.

After all, my fellow citizens, it is neither extraordinary or unexpected, that the constitution offered to your consideration, should meet with opposition. It is the nature of man to pursue his own interest, in preference to the public good; and I do not mean to make any personal reflection, when I add, that it is the interest of a very numerous, powerful, and respectable body to counteract and destroy the excellent work produced by the late convention. All the offices of government, and all the appointments for the administration of justice and the collection of the public revenue, which are transferred from the individual to the aggregate sovereignty of the states, will necessarily turn the stream of influence and emolument into a new channel. Every person therefore, who either enjoys, or expects to enjoy, a place of profit under the present establishment, will object to the proposed innovation; not, in truth, because it is injurious to the liberties of his country, but because it affects his schemes of wealth and consequence. I will confess indeed, that I am not a blind admirer of this plan of government, and that there are some parts of it, which if my wish had prevailed, would certainly have been altered. But, when I reflect how widely men differ in their opinions, and that every man (and the observation applies likewise to every state) has an equal pretension

---

[2] tax on imports

to assert his own, I am satisfied that any thing nearer to perfection could not have been accomplished. If there are errors, it should be remembered, that the seeds of reformation are sown in the work itself, and the concurrence of two thirds of the congress may at any time introduce alterations and amendments. Regarding it then, in every point of view, with a candid and disinterested mind, I am bold to assert, that it is the best form of government which has ever been offered to the world.

The Federal Farmer IV

October 12, 1787

The Antifederalist Federal Farmer, without mentioning James Wilson by name (Document 10), criticized the claim of his State House speech that a bill of rights is unnecessary and dangerous. The Federal Farmer argued that the provisions of Article I, Sections 9 and 10 of the Constitution (Appendix D) were a partial bill of rights—see the restriction on ex post facto laws—so why not either drop such protection for rights or go the whole distance and itemize a bill of rights that incudes "other essential rights"?

The Federal Farmer was concerned that the Constitution contained within itself the potentiality to become a consolidated government despite Wilson's argument that the Constitution only bestowed powers that were clearly enumerated. If the latter were the case, then Wilson would be arguing that the framers of the Constitution created a confederacy with expressly delegated powers. How strange would that be, since the point of the Constitutional Convention was to provide remedies for the defects of just such a form of government. The Federal Farmer thought the framers created a government and not simply a revision of a confederation. Thus, the government needed a comprehensive bill of rights, since the Constitution contained the seeds of a general government operating with unlimited powers.

SOURCE: *The Federalist and Other Constitutional Papers by Hamilton, Jay, Madison and Other Statesmen of Their Time*, E. H. Scott, ed. (Chicago: Albert, Scott & Company, 1894), 867–874; https://goo.gl/xbm7mw.

... It is said, that when the people make a constitution, and delegate powers that all powers not delegated by them to those who govern is [sic] reserved in the people; and that the people, in the present case, have reserved in themselves, and in their state governments, every right and power not expressly given by the federal Constitution to those who shall administer the national government. It is said, on the other hand, that the people, when they make a constitution, yield all power not expressly reserved to themselves. The truth is, in either case, it is mere matter of opinion, and men usually take either side of the argument, as will best answer their purposes: But the general presumption being, that men who govern, will, in doubtful cases, construe laws and constitutions most favorably for increasing their own powers; all wise and prudent people, in forming constitutions, have drawn the line, and carefully described the powers parted with and the powers reserved. By the state constitutions, certain rights have been reserved in the people; or rather, they have been recognized and established in such a manner, that state legislatures are bound to respect them, and to make no laws infringing upon them. The state legislatures are obliged to take notice of the bills of rights of their respective states. The bills of rights, and the state constitutions, are fundamental compacts only between those who govern, and the people of the same state.

In the year 1788 the people of the United States make a federal Constitution, which is a fundamental compact between them and their federal rulers; these rulers, in the nature of things, cannot be bound to take notice of any other compact. It would be absurd for them, in making laws, to look over thirteen, fifteen, or twenty state constitutions, to see what rights are established as fundamental, and must not be infringed upon, in making laws in the society. It is true, they would be bound to do it if the people, in their federal compact, should refer to the state constitutions, recognize all parts not inconsistent with the federal constitution, and direct their federal rulers to take notice of them accordingly; but this is not the case, as the plan stands proposed at present; and it is absurd, to suppose so unnatural an idea is intended or implied, I think my opinion is not only founded in reason, but I think it is supported by the report of the convention itself. If there are a number of rights established by the state constitutions, and which will remain sacred, and the general government is bound to take notice of them—it must take notice of one as well as another; and if unnecessary to recognize or establish one by the federal Constitution, it would be unnecessary to recognize or establish another by it. If the federal Constitution is to be construed so far in connection with the state constitutions, as to leave the trial by jury in civil causes, for instance, secured; on the same principles it would have left the trial by jury in criminal causes, the benefits of the writ of habeas corpus, &c. secured; they all stand on the same footing; they are the common rights of Americans, and have been recognized by the state constitutions: But the convention found it necessary to recognize or re-establish the benefits of that writ, and the jury trial in criminal cases. As to EXPOST FACTO laws, the convention has done the same in one case, and gone further in another. It is part of the compact between the people of each state and their rulers, that no EXPOST FACTO laws shall be made. But the Convention, by Art. I Sect. 10 have put a sanction upon this part even of the state compacts. In fact, the 9th and 10th Sections in Art. 1. in the proposed Constitution, are no more nor less, than a partial bill of rights; they establish certain principles as part of the compact upon which the federal legislators and officers can never infringe. It is here wisely stipulated, that the federal legislature shall never pass a bill of attainder, or EXPOST FACTO law; that no tax shall be laid on articles exported, &c. The establishing of one right implies the necessity of establishing another and similar one.

On the whole, the position appears to me to be undeniable, that this bill of rights ought to be carried farther, and some other principles established, as a part of this fundamental compact between the people of the United States and their federal rulers.

It is true, we are not disposed to differ much, at present, about religion; but when we are making a constitution, it is to be hoped, for ages and millions yet unborn, why not establish the free exercise of religion, as a part of the national compact. There are other essential rights, which we have justly understood to be the rights of freemen; as freedom from hasty and unreasonable search warrants, warrants not founded on oath, and not issued with due caution, for searching and seizing men's papers, property, and persons. The trials by jury in civil causes, it is said, varies so much in the several states, that no words could be found for the uniform establishment of it. If so the federal legislation will not be able to establish it by any general laws. I confess I am of opinion it may be established, but not in that beneficial manner in which we may enjoy it, for the reasons before mentioned. When I speak of the jury trial of the vicinage,[1] or the trial of the fact in the neighborhood. I do not lay so much stress upon the circumstance of our being tried by our neighbors: in this enlightened country men may be probably impartially tried by those who do not live very near them: but the trial of facts in the neighborhood is of great importance in other respects. Nothing can be more essential than the cross-examining witnesses, and generally before the triers of the facts in question. The common people can establish facts with much more ease with oral than written evidence; when trials of facts are removed to a distance from the homes of the parties and witnesses, oral evidence becomes intolerably expensive, and the parties must depend on written evidence, which to

---

[1] vicinity

the common people is expensive and almost useless; it must be frequently taken ex-parte,[2] and but very seldom leads to the proper discovery of truth.

The trial by jury is very important in another point of view. It is essential in every free country, that common people should have a part and share of influence, in the judicial as well as in the legislative department. To hold open to them the offices of senators, judges, and offices to fill which an expensive education is required, cannot answer any valuable purposes for them; they are not in a situation to be brought forward and to fill those offices; these, and most other offices of any considerable importance, will be occupied by the few. The few, the well born, &c. as Mr. Adams calls them, in judicial decisions as well as in legislation, are generally disposed, and very naturally too, to favor those of their own description....

---

[2] from or on behalf of only one of the parties

Richard Henry Lee to Edmund Randolph

October 16, 1787

R ichard Henry Lee was a powerful Virginia and national politician who numerous scholars argue was the author of the Federal Farmer essays (Document 11). Three points are important in this letter. First, Lee wrote to Edmund Randolph, Governor of Virginia, who had declined to sign the Constitution a month before and was under considerable pressure from all sides during the ratification process. Second, in many ways, Lee anticipated the important debate between Thomas Jefferson and James Madison over what rights were essential (Documents 16, 20, and 21). It is instructive that the first three of the fourteen rights on Lee's list are exactly the same as are on Madison and Jefferson's list of essential rights. Third, Lee's fourteen proposed declarations are not antagonistic to the institutional framework of the Constitution. So, not all Antifederalists were totally opposed to the Constitution. What they wanted were greater assurances that the proposed Constitution would not become a consolidated system. For this reason, they wanted a bill of rights.

Lee originally presented the alterations to the proposed Constitution in one continuous paragraph; to assist the reader, we have broken the paragraph into fourteen thematic divisions. Contra James Wilson (Document 10), Lee articulates the traditional argument that a bill of rights is needed to protect the people from the tyranny of the few.

SOURCE: *The American Museum or Repository of Ancient and Modern Fugitive Pieces, etc., Prose and Poetical* for July 1787, vol. II, no. 1 (Philadelphia: Matthew Carey, 1789), 553–558; https://goo.gl/H5jnWL.

It having been found from universal experience, that the most expressed declarations and reservations are necessary to protect the just rights and liberty of mankind from the silent powerful and ever active conspiracy of those who govern; and it appearing to be the sense of the good people of America, by the various bills or declarations of rights whereon the government of the greater number of states are founded: that such precautions are necessary to restrain and regulate the exercise of the great powers given to the rulers. In conformity with these principles, and from respect for the public sentiment on this subject, it is submitted, that the new Constitution proposed for the government of the United States be bottomed upon a declaration or bill of rights, clearly and precisely stating the principles upon which this social compact is founded, to wit:

(1) that the rights of conscience in matters of religion ought not to be violated,

(2) that the freedom of the press shall be secured,

(3) that the trial by jury in criminal and civil cases, and the modes prescribed by the common law for the safety of life in criminal prosecutions shall be held sacred,

(4) that standing armies in times of peace are dangerous to liberty, and ought not to be permitted unless assented to by two-thirds of the members composing each house of the legislature under the new Constitution,

(5) that the elections should be free and frequent,

(6) that the right administration of justice should be secured by the independence of the judges,

(7) that excessive bail, excessive fines, or cruel and unusual punishments should not be demanded or inflicted,

(8) that the right of the people to assemble peaceably for the purpose of petitioning the legislature shall not be prevented,

(9) that the citizens shall not be exposed to unreasonable searches, seizure of their persons, houses, papers or property,

(10) and it is necessary for the good of society, that the administration of government be conducted with all possible maturity of judgment, for which reason it has been the practice of civilized nations and so determined by every state in the Union, that a council of state or privy council should be appointed to advise and assist in the arduous business assigned to the executive power. Therefore let the new Constitution be so amended as to admit the appointment of a privy council to consist of eleven members chosen by the president, but responsible for the advice they may give. For which purpose the advice given shall be entered in a council book, and signed by the giver in all affairs of great moment, and that the counselors act under an oath of office. In order to prevent the dangerous blending of the legislative and executive powers, and to secure responsibility, the privy, and not the senate, shall be joined with the president in the appointment of all officers civil and military under the new Constitution, that the Constitution be so altered as not to admit the creation of a vice president, when duties as assigned may

be discharged by the privy council, except in the instance of proceedings in the senate, which may be supplied by a speaker chosen from the body of senators by themselves as usual, that so may be avoided the establishment of a great officer of state, who is sometimes to be joined with the legislature, and sometimes administer the government, rendering responsibility difficult, besides giving unjust and needless pre-eminence to that state from whence this officer may have come,

(11) that such parts of the new Constitution be amended as provide imperfectly for the trial of criminals by a jury of the vicinage, and so supply the omission of a jury trial in civil causes or disputes about property between individuals, whereby the common law is directed, and as generally it is secured by the several state constitutions,

(12) that such parts of the new Constitution be amended as permit the vexatious and oppressive callings of citizens from their own country, and all controversies between citizens of different states and between citizens and foreigners, to be tried in a far distant court, and as it may be without a jury, whereby in a multitude of cases, the circumstances of distance and expense, may compel numbers to submit to the most unjust and ill founded demand,

(13) that in order to secure the rights of the people more effectually from violation, the power and respectability of the House of Representatives be increased, by increasing the number of delegates to that house where the popular interest must chiefly depend for protection,

(14) that the Constitution be so amended as to increase the number of votes necessary to determine questions in cases where a bare majority may be seduced by strong motives of interest to injure and oppress the minority of the community as in commercial regulations, where advantage may be taken of circumstances to ordain rigid and premature laws that will in effect amount to monopolies, to the great impoverishment of those states whose peculiar situation expose them to such injuries.

An Old Whig IV

October 27, 1787

A n Old Whig, a prominent Pennsylvania Antifederalist whose identity is unknown, contended that the Constitution contains the potential to produce a consolidated government ruling over one large territory. Reflecting received opinion, he argued that such a government, would not remain republican. The only hope for republican government was to form a confederacy of the states. (It was this view that James Madison contended against in the Constitutional Convention, the Virginia Ratifying Convention [Document 17], and Federalist 10. He offered an alternative "science of politics," accepting faction, which the republican tradition had deplored, as essential to preserving liberty in an extended republic.) The Old Whig also argued that given the power of the proposed government, a bill of rights was essential. He buttressed his case by appealing to the precedents in English history for such explicit guarantees of rights. In addition to appealing to the British tradition of due process, he also appealed to the new American claim to "natural liberty." During the campaign over adoption of the Constitution, the appeal to "natural liberty" had a greater impact on the electorate than an appeal to the British tradition. It certainly had a greater impact on Madison in the First Congress (Document 22).

SOURCE: From the Independent gazetteer: This is certainly a very important crisis to the people of America. Philadelphia, 1787. The Library of Congress; https://goo.gl/xYb6tS.

... It is beyond a doubt that the new federal Constitution, if adopted, will in a great measure destroy, if it does not totally annihilate, the separate governments of the several states. We shall, in effect become one great republic. Every measure of importance, will be continental. What will be the consequence of this? One thing is evident, that no republic of so great a magnitude, ever did, or ever can exist. But a few years elapsed, from the time in which ancient Rome extended her dominion beyond the bounds of Italy, until the downfall of her republic; and all political writers agree, that a republican government can exist only in a narrow territory: but a confederacy of different republics has, in many instances, existed and flourished for a long time together. The celebrated Helvetian League,[1] which exists at the moment in full vigor, and with unimpaired strength, whilst its origin may be traced to the confines of antiquity, is one, among many examples on this head; and at the same time furnishes an eminent proof of how much less importance it is that the constituent parts of a confederacy of republics may be rightly framed than it is that the confederacy itself should be rightly organized; for hardly any two of the Swiss cantons have the same form of government, and they are almost equally divided in their religious principles, which have so often rent asunder the firmest establishments.

A confederacy of republics must be the establishment in America, or we must cease altogether to retain the republican form of government. From the moment we become one great republic, either in form or substance, the period is very shortly removed, when we shall sink first into monarchy, and then into despotism. If there were no other fault in the proposed constitution, it must sink by its own weight. The continent of North America can no more be governed by one republic, than the fabled Atlas could support the heavens. Is it not worthy a few months labor to attempt rescuing this country from the despotism, which at this moment holds the best and fairest regions of the earth in thraldom and wretchedness? To attempt the forming a plan of confederation, which may enable us at once to support our continental union with vigor and efficacy, and to maintain the rights of the separate states and the invaluable liberty of the subject? These ideas of political felicity to some people may seem like the visions of a utopian fantasy; and I am persuaded that some amongst us have as little disposition to realize them, as they have to recollect the principles, which inspired us in our revolt from Great Britain. But there is at least, this consolation in aiming at excellence, that if we do not obtain our object, we can make considerable progress toward it.

The science of politics has very seldom had fair play. So much of passion, interest and temporary prospects of gain are mixed in the pursuit that a government has been much oftener established with a view to the particular advantages or necessities of a few individuals than to the permanent good of society. If the men who at different times have been entrusted to form plans of government for the world had been really actuated by no other views than a regard to the public good, the condition of human nature in all ages would have been widely different, from that which has been exhibited

---

[1] A confederacy of Swiss cantons that formed during the 13th century and collapsed in 1798.

to us in history. In this country perhaps we are possessed of more than our share of political virtue. If we will exercise a little patience, and bestow our best endeavors on the business, I do not think it impossible, that we may yet form a federal constitution, much superior to any form of government, which has ever existed in the world; but whenever this important work shall be accomplished, I venture to pronounce that it will not be done without a careful attention to the framing of a bill of rights.

Much has been said and written, on the subject of a bill of rights; possibly without sufficient attention to the necessity of conveying distinct and precise ideas of the true meaning of a bill of rights. Your readers, I hope, will excuse me, if I conclude this letter with an attempt to throw some light on this subject.

Men when they enter into society yield up a part of their natural liberty, for the sake of being protected by government. If they yield up all their natural rights, they are absolute slaves to their governors. If they yield up less than is necessary, the government is so feeble that it cannot protect them. To yield up so much, as is necessary for the purposes of government; and to retain all beyond what is necessary is the great point, which ought, if possible, to be attained in the formation of a constitution. At the same time that by these means, the liberty of the subject is secured, the government is really strengthened; because wherever the subject is convinced that nothing more is required from him than what is necessary for the good of the community, he yields a cheerful obedience, which is more useful than the constrained service of slaves. To define what portion of his natural liberty, the subject shall at the time be entitled to retain is one great end of a bill of rights. To these may be added in a bill of rights some particular engagements of protection, on the part of the government. Without such a bill of rights firmly securing the privileges of the subject, the government is always in danger of degenerating into tyranny; for it is certainly true, that "in establishing the powers of government, the rulers are invested with every right and authority, which is not in explicit terms reserved."[2] Hence it is that we find the patriots, in all ages of the world, so very solicitous to obtain explicit engagements from their rulers, stipulating expressly for the preservation of particular rights and privileges.

In different nations, we find different grants or reservations of privileges appealed to in the struggles between the rulers and the people, many of which in the different nations of Europe have long since been swallowed up and lost by time, or destroyed by the arbitrary hand of power. In England we find the

---

[2] See Document 10, second paragraph.

people, with the barons at their head, exacting a solemn resignation of their rights from King John, in their celebrated Magna Carta,[3] which has many times renewed in Parliament, during the reigns of his successors. The petition of rights[4] was afterwards consented to by Charles the First, and contained a declaration of the liberties of the people. The habeas corpus act,[5] after the restoration of Charles the Second, the bill of rights,[6] which was obtained from the Prince and Princess of Orange on their accession to the throne, and the act of settlement,[7] at the accession of the Hanover family, are other instances to show the care and watchfulness of that nation to improve every opportunity of the reign of a weak prince, or the revolution in their government, to obtain the most explicit declaration in favor of their liberties. In like manner the people of the country, at the revolution, having all power in their own hands, in forming the constitutions of several states, took care to secure themselves by bills of rights, so as to prevent, as far as possible, the encroachments of their future rulers upon the rights of the people. Some of these rights are said to be unalienable, such as the rights of conscience: yet even these have been often invaded, where they have not been carefully secured by express and solemn bills and declarations in their favor.

Before we establish a government, whose acts will be THE SUPREME LAW OF THE LAND, and whose power will extend to almost every case without exception, we ought carefully to guard ourselves by a BILL OF RIGHTS, against the invasion of those liberties which it is essential for us to retain, which it is of no real use to government to strip us of; but which in the course of human events have been too often insulted with all the wantonness of an idle barbarity.

---

[3] Signed in 1215

[4] The Petition of Right, 1628, was a statement by Parliament of the rights of Englishmen.

[5] Passed by Parliament in 1679, the Habeas Corpus Act defined the common law right of freedom from arbitrary imprisonment.

[6] An act of Parliament passed in 1689 declaring the rights of Englishmen, following the abdication of Charles II and the ascension to the throne by William and Mary, "the Prince and Princess of Orange."

[7] An act of Parliament passed in 1701, which established that future Kings or Queens would be Protestant.

Brutus II

November 1, 1787

In the second of sixteen essays that he published in the New York Journal, the prominent New York Antifederalist, Brutus (thought by some to be Melancton Smith, an experienced New York politician) concurred with the arguments of George Mason and Richard Henry Lee (Documents 9 and 12). There was no doubt in their minds that the new plan of government had the potential to concentrate power in the hands of the few. There was also a remarkable uniformity in the specific individual rights they thought needed protection: rights of conscience, freedom of the press, freedom of association, no unreasonable searches and seizures, trial by jury in civil cases, and no cruel and unusual punishment.

In his second essay, Brutus revisited "the merits" of the argument in his first essay, Brutus I, "that to reduce the thirteen states into one government, would prove the destruction of your liberties." Again anticipating The Federalist, Brutus argued, "when a building is to be erected which is intended to stand for ages, the foundation should be firmly laid." But the foundation of the Constitution was poorly laid, he thought, because it lacked a declaration of rights "expressly reserving to the people such of their essential natural rights, as are not necessary to be parted with." He rejected as "specious" the arguments of an unnamed framer's State House speech (James Wilson, Document 10) as to why a bill of rights is unnecessary: after all, "the powers, rights, and authority, granted to the general government by this Constitution, are as complete, with respect to every object to which they extend, as that of any state government." Furthermore, Brutus asked, why did the framers secure certain rights in Article I, Section 9, "but omitted others of more importance"? This is similar to the appeal to "natural liberty" by Old Whig (Document 13). What was emerging in this Antifederalist literature was a coherent case for a bill of rights to constrain a potentially runaway national government that would concentrate all power in a district ten miles square.

SOURCE: *Debates and Proceedings of the Convention of the Commonwealth of Massachusetts Held in the Year 1788 and Which Finally Ratified the Constitution of the United States* (Boston: William White Printer to the Commonwealth, 1856), 378–384; https://goo.gl/dkYHMi.

To the Citizens of the State of New York.

I flatter myself that my last address established this position, that to reduce the thirteen States into one government, would prove the destruction of your liberties.

But lest this truth should be doubted by some, I will now proceed to consider its merits.

Though it should be admitted that the argument[s] against reducing all the states into one consolidated government are not sufficient fully to establish this point; yet they will, at least, justify this conclusion that in forming a constitution for such a country, great care should be taken to limit and define its powers, adjust its parts, and guard against an abuse of authority. How far attention has been paid to these objects, shall be the subject of future enquiry. When a building is to be erected which is intended to stand for ages, the foundation should be firmly laid. The Constitution proposed to your acceptance, is designed not for yourselves alone, but for generations yet unborn. The principles, therefore, upon which the social compact is founded, ought to have been clearly and precisely stated, and the most express and full declaration of rights to have been made—but on this subject there is almost an entire silence.

If we may collect the sentiments of the people of America, from their own most solemn declarations, they hold this truth as self-evident, that all men are by nature free. No one man, therefore, or any class of men, have a right, by the law of nature, or of God, to assume or exercise authority over their fellows. The origin of society then is to be sought, not in any natural right which one man has to exercise authority over another, but in the united consent of those who associate. The mutual wants of men, at first dictated the propriety of forming societies; and when they were established, protection and defense pointed out the necessity of instituting government. In a state of nature every individual pursues his own interest; in this pursuit it frequently happened that the possessions or enjoyments of one were sacrificed to the views and designs of another; thus the weak were a prey to the strong, the simple and unwary were subject to impositions from those who were more crafty and designing. In this state of things, every individual was insecure; common interest therefore directed that government should be established in which the force of the whole community should be collected, and under such directions, as to protect and defend every one who composed it. The common good, therefore, is the end of civil government, and common consent, the foundation on which it is established. To effect this end, it was necessary that a certain portion of natural liberty should be surrendered in order that what remained should be preserved: how great a proportion of natural freedom is necessary to be yielded by individuals when they submit to government, I shall not now enquire. So much, however, must be given up, as will be sufficient to enable those to whom the administration of the government is committed to establish laws for the promoting the happiness of the community, and to carry those laws into effect. But it is not necessary for this purpose that individuals should relinquish all their natural rights. Some are of such a nature that they cannot be surrendered. Of this kind are the rights of conscience, the right of enjoying and defending life, etc. Others are not necessary to be resigned in order to attain the end for which government is instituted, these therefore ought not to be given up. To surrender them, would counteract the very end of government, to wit, the common good. From these observations it appears, that in forming a government on its true principles, the foundation should be laid in the manner I before stated, by expressly reserving to the people such of their essential natural rights as are not necessary to be parted with. The same reasons which at first induced mankind to associate and institute government will operate to influence them to observe this precaution. If they had been disposed to conform themselves to the rule of immutable righteousness, government would not have been requisite. It was because one part exercised fraud, oppression, and violence on the other, that men came together, and agreed that certain rules should be formed, to regulate the conduct of all, and the power of the whole community lodged in the hands of rulers to enforce an obedience to them. But rulers have the same propensities as other men; they are as likely to use the power with which they are vested for private purposes, and to the injury and oppression of those over whom they are placed, as individuals in a state of nature are to injure and oppress one another. It is therefore as proper that bounds should be set to their authority, as that government should have at first been instituted to restrain private injuries.

This principle, which seems so evidently founded in the reason and nature of things, is confirmed by universal experience. Those who have governed, have been found in all ages ever active to enlarge their powers and abridge the public liberty. This has induced the people in all countries, where any sense of freedom remained, to fix barriers against the encroachments of their rulers. The country from which we have derived our origin, is an eminent example of this. Their Magna Charta[1] and Bill of Rights[2] have long been the boast,

---

[1] A charter signed in 1215 by English barons and King John specifying certain limits on the power of the king
[2] An act of Parliament in 1689 that specified limits on the power of the crown

as well as the security, of that nation. I need say no more, I presume, to an American than that this principle is a fundamental one in all the constitutions of our own states; there is not one of them but what is either founded on a declaration or bill of rights, or has certain express reservation of rights interwoven in the body of them. From this it appears that at a time when the pulse of liberty beat high and when an appeal was made to the people to form constitutions for the government of themselves, it was their universal sense that such declarations should make a part of their frames of government. It is therefore the more astonishing that this grand security to the rights of the people is not to be found in this Constitution.

It has been said, in answer to this objection, that such declaration[s] of rights, however requisite they might be in the constitutions of the states, are not necessary in the general Constitution, because "in the former case, every thing which is not reserved is given, but in the latter the reverse of the proposition prevails, and every thing which is not given is reserved."[3] It requires but little attention to discover that this mode of reasoning is rather specious than solid. The powers, rights, and authority granted to the general government by this Constitution, are as complete, with respect to every object to which they extend, as that of any state government—it reaches to every thing which concerns human happiness—life, liberty, and property are under its control. There is the same reason, therefore, that the exercise of power, in this case, should be restrained within proper limits, as in that of the state governments. To set this matter in a clear light, permit me to instance some of the articles of the bills of rights of the individual states, and apply them to the case in question.

For the security of life, in criminal prosecutions, the bills of rights of most of the states have declared, that no man shall be held to answer for a crime until he is made fully acquainted with the charge brought against him; he shall not be compelled to accuse, or furnish evidence against himself—the witnesses against him shall be brought face to face, and he shall be fully heard by himself or counsel. That it is essential to the security of life and liberty, that trial of facts be in the vicinity where they happen. Are not provisions of this kind as necessary in the general government, as in that of a particular state? The powers vested in the new Congress extend in many cases to life; they are authorized to provide for the punishment of a variety of capital crimes, and no restraint is laid upon them in its exercise, save only that "the trial of all crimes, except in cases of impeachment, shall be by jury; and such trial shall

[3] Document 10

be in the state where the said crimes shall have been committed."[4] No man is secure of a trial in the county where he is charged to have committed a crime; he may be brought from Niagara to New York, or carried from Kentucky to Richmond for trial for an offence supposed to be committed. What security is there that a man shall be furnished with a full and plain description of the charges against him? That he shall be allowed to produce all proof he can in his favor? That he shall see the witnesses against him face to face, or that he shall be fully heard in his own defense by himself or counsel?

For the security of liberty it has been declared, "that excessive bail should not be required, nor excessive fines imposed, nor cruel or unusual punishments inflicted—that all warrants, without oath or affirmation, to search suspected places, or seize any person, his papers or property, are grievous and oppressive."[5]

These provisions are as necessary under the general government as under that of the individual states; for the power of the former is as complete to the purpose of requiring bail, imposing fines, inflicting punishments, granting search warrants, and seizing persons, papers, or property, in certain cases, as the other.

For the purpose of securing the property of the citizens, it is declared by all the states, "that in all controversies at law, respecting property, the ancient mode of trial by jury is one of the best securities of the rights of the people, and ought to remain sacred and inviolable."[6]

Does not the same necessity exist of reserving this right, under this national compact, as in that of these states? Yet nothing is said respecting it. In the bills of rights of the states it is declared, that a well regulated militia is the proper and natural defense of a free government—that as standing armies in time of peace are dangerous, they are not to be kept up, and that the military should be kept under strict subordination to and controlled by the civil power.

The same security is as necessary in this Constitution, and much more so; for the general government will have the sole power to raise and to pay armies, and are under no control in the exercise of it; yet nothing of this is to be found in this new system.

I might proceed to instance a number of other rights, which were as

---

[4] Constitution, Article III, section 2
[5] Language taken from amendments to the Constitution proposed at the Virginia ratifying convention
[6] North Carolina Constitution

necessary to be reserved, such as that elections should be free, that the liberty of the press should be held sacred; but the instances adduced are sufficient to prove that this argument is without foundation. Besides, it is evident, that the reason here assigned was not the true one, why the framers of this Constitution omitted a bill of rights; if it had been, they would not have made certain reservations, while they totally omitted others of more importance. We find they have, in the ninth section of the first article, declared, that the writ of habeas corpus shall not be suspended, unless in cases of rebellion— that no bill of attainder or ex-post facto law shall be passed—that no title of nobility shall be granted by the United States, &c. If every thing which is not given is reserved, what propriety is there in these exceptions? Does this Constitution anywhere grant the power of suspending the habeas corpus, to make ex-post facto laws, pass bills of attainder, or grant titles of nobility? It certainly does not in express terms. The only answer that can be given is that these are implied in the general powers granted. With equal truth it may be said that all the powers, which the bills of right guard against the abuse of, are contained or implied in the general ones granted by this constitution.

So far it is from being true, that a bill of rights is less necessary in the general Constitution than in those of the states, the contrary is evidently the fact. This system, if it is possible for the people of America to accede to it, will be an original compact; and being the last will, in the nature of things, vacate every former agreement inconsistent with it. For it being a plan of government received and ratified by the whole people, all other forms, which are in existence at the time of its adoption, must yield to it. This is expressed in positive and unequivocal terms, in the sixth article, "That this constitution and the laws of the United States, which shall be made in pursuance thereof, and all treaties made, or which shall be made, under the authority of the United States, shall be the supreme law of the land; and the judges in every state shall be bound thereby, any thing in the constitution, or laws of any state, to the contrary notwithstanding.

"The senators and representatives before-mentioned, and the members of the several state legislatures, and all executive and judicial officers, both of the United States, and of the several states, shall be bound, by oath or affirmation, to support this constitution."[7]

It is therefore not only necessarily implied thereby but positively expressed that the different state constitutions are repealed and entirely done away, so far as they are inconsistent with this, with the laws which shall be

---

[7] Also Article VI

made in pursuance thereof, or with treaties made, or which shall be made, under the authority of the United States; of what avail will the constitutions of the respective states be to preserve the rights of its citizens? Should they be plead, the answer would be, the Constitution of the United States and the laws made in pursuance thereof is the supreme law, and all legislatures and judicial officers, whether of the general or state governments are bound by oath to support it. No privilege reserved by the bills of rights, or secured by the state government, can limit the power granted by this or restrain any laws made in pursuance of it. It stands therefore on its own bottom, and must receive a construction by itself without any reference to any other—and hence it was of the highest importance that the most precise and express declarations and reservations of rights should have been made.

This will appear the more necessary, when it is considered that not only the Constituion and laws made in pursuance thereof, but all treaties made, or which shall be made, under the authority of the United States, are the supreme law of the land, and supersede the constitutions of all the states. The power to make treaties is vested in the president by and with the advice and consent of two thirds of the senate. I do not find any limitation, or restriction, to the exercise of this power. The most important article in any constitution may therefore be repealed, even without a legislative act. Ought not a government vested with such extensive and indefinite authority to have been restricted by a declaration of rights? It certainly ought.

So clear a point is this that I cannot help suspecting that persons who attempt to persuade people that such reservations were less necessary under this Constitution than under those of the states are wilfully endeavoring to deceive and to lead you into an absolute state of vassalage.

DOCUMENT 15

The Dissent of the Minority of the Convention of Pennsylvania

December 18, 1787

Going into the Pennsylvania Ratifying Convention, the expectation was that forty-six delegates would vote in favor and twenty-three against adoption of the proposed Constitution. Indeed, Pennsylvania voted to ratify the Constitution, 46–23. The report issued by the twenty-three Pennsylvania opponents—the Pennsylvania Minority—had no impact on the outcome in Pennsylvania, but it did have a considerable impact on the subsequent campaign over ratification. The report proposed two alterations. On the one hand, the Pennsylvania Minority called for amendments that would re-establish the principles of the Articles of Confederation. These were what James Madison would later argue to be unfriendly to the Constitution (Documents 17, 21 and 22). On the other hand, the Pennsylvania Minority proposed that a declaration of rights be annexed to the Constitution. What became the first, fourth, fifth, sixth, seventh, and eighth amendments to the Constitution were addressed in their list. This distinction between unfriendly structural amendments on the one hand and a friendly bill of rights on the other became critical in the Virginia and New York Ratifying Conventions as well as in the First Congress (Documents 17, 18, 22).

Most notably, the right of conscience led the list of rights to be preserved. Both sides in the debate agreed on the primacy of the right to conscience. Concerning the seventh—the right to bear arms—eight out of the thirteen original states included a right to bear arms for self-defense and service in the militia. James Madison raised this connection in the First Congress (Document 22). What is fascinating and unique about the Pennsylvania Bill of Rights (Document 5), and confirmed in this report, is the claim that the people have the right to bear arms for the purpose of "killing game," a right to bear arms not directly connected to the militia.

SOURCE: Nathaniel Breading, Eleazer Oswald, et. al., *The Address and reasons of dissent of the minority of the convention, of the state of Pennsylvania, to their constituents* (Philadelphia: Printed by E. Oswald, 1787); Constitutional Convention Broadside Collection, Library of Congress, https://goo.gl/MB98fL.

... The Convention met, and the same disposition was soon manifested in considering the proposed Constitution, that had been exhibited in every other stage of the business. We were prohibited by an express vote of the Convention, from taking any question on the separate articles of the plan, and reduced to the necessity of adopting or rejecting in toto. 'Tis true the majority permitted us to debate on each article, but restrained us from proposing amendments. They also determined not to permit us to enter on the minutes our reasons of dissent against any of the articles, nor even on the final question our reasons of dissent against the whole. Thus situated we entered on the examination of the proposed system of government, and found it to be such as we could not adopt, without, as we conceived, surrendering up your dearest rights. We offered our objections to the convention, and opposed those parts of the plan, which, in our opinion, would be injurious to you, in the best manner we were able; and closed our arguments by offering the following propositions to the convention.

1. The right of conscience shall be held inviolable; and neither the legislative, executive, nor judicial powers of the United States shall have authority to alter, abrogate, or infringe any part of the constitution of the several states, which provide for the preservation of liberty in matters of religion.

2. That in controversies respecting property, and in suits between man and man, trial by jury shall remain as heretofore, as well in the federal courts, as in those of the several states.

3. That in all capital and criminal prosecutions, a man has a right to demand the cause and nature of his accusation, as well in the federal courts, as in those of the several states; to be heard by himself and his counsel; to be confronted with the accusers and witnesses; to call for evidence in his favor, and a speedy trial by an impartial jury of his vicinage, without whose unanimous consent, he cannot be found guilty, nor can he be compelled to give evidence against himself; and that no man be deprived of his liberty, except by the law of the land or the judgment of his peers.

4. That excessive bail ought not to be required, nor excessive fines imposed, nor cruel nor unusual punishments inflicted.

5. That warrants unsupported by evidence, whereby any officer or messenger may be commanded or required to search suspected places, or to seize any person or persons, his or their property, not

particularly described, are grievous and oppressive, and shall not be granted either by the magistrates of the federal government or others.

6. That the people have a right to the freedom of speech, of writing and publishing their sentiments, therefore, the freedom of the press shall not be restrained by any law of the United States.

7. That the people have a right to bear arms for the defense of themselves and their own state, or the United States, or for the purpose of killing game; and no law shall be passed for disarming the people or any of them, unless for crimes committed, or real danger of public injury from individuals; and as standing armies in the time of peace are dangerous to liberty, they ought not to be kept up; and that the military shall be kept under strict subordination to and be governed by the civil powers.

8. The inhabitants of the several states shall have liberty to fowl and hunt in seasonable times, on the lands they hold, and on all other lands in the United States not enclosed, and in like manner to fish in all navigable waters, and others not private property, without being restrained therein by any laws to be passed by the legislature of the United States.

9. That no law shall be passed to restrain the legislatures of the several states from enacting laws for imposing taxes, except imposts and duties on goods imported or exported, and that no taxes, except imposts and duties upon goods imported and exported, and postage on letters shall be levied by the authority of Congress.

10. That the House of Representatives be properly increased in number; that elections shall remain free; that the several states shall have power to regulate the elections for senators and representatives, without being controlled either directly or indirectly by an interference on the part of the Congress; and that elections of representatives be annual.

11. That the power of organizing, arming, and disciplining the militia (the manner of disciplining the militia to be prescribed by Congress) remain with the individual states, and that Congress shall not have authority to call or march any of the militia out of their own state, without the consent of such state, and for such length of time only as such state shall agree. That the sovereignty, freedom, and independency of the several states shall be retained,

and every power, jurisdiction, and right which is not by this
constitution expressly delegated to the United States in Congress
assembled.

12. That the legislative, executive, and judicial powers be kept separate;
    and to this end that a constitutional council be appointed, to advise
    and assist the president, who shall be responsible for the advice
    they give, hereby the senators would be relieved from almost
    constant attendance; and also that the judges be made completely
    independent.

13. That no treaty which shall be directly opposed to the existing laws
    of the United States in Congress assembled shall be valid until
    such laws shall be repealed, or made conformable to such treaty;
    neither shall any treaties be valid which are in contradiction to
    the Constitution of the United States, or the constitutions of the
    several states.

14. That the judiciary power of the United States shall be confined to
    cases affecting ambassadors, other public ministers and consuls;
    to cases of admiralty and maritime jurisdiction; to controversies to
    which the United States shall be a party; to controversies between
    two or more states—between a state and citizens of different
    states—between citizens claiming lands under grants of different
    states; and between a state or the citizens thereof and foreign states,
    and in criminal cases, to such only as are expressly enumerated in
    the constitution, and that the United States in Congress assembled
    shall not have power to enact laws, which shall alter the laws
    of descents and distribution of the effects of deceased persons,
    the titles of lands or goods, or the regulation of contracts in the
    individual states....

Thomas Jefferson to James Madison

December 20, 1787

*I*n October 1787, James Madison sent a copy of the signed Constitution to Thomas Jefferson in Paris, where he was serving as the Ambassador to the Court of Louis XVI. In his letter, Madison explained that the Constitution was a vital improvement in structure and power over the Articles of Confederation. He wished, however, that more checks and balances had been included. In this response to Madison, Jefferson first summarized what he liked about the proposed document. He was "captivated" by what the delegates to the Convention called the partly national, partly federal compromise. Jefferson then turned to "what I do not like." He was troubled by two omissions. He listed six rights that ought to be stated "clearly and without sophisms." And he wanted the President limited to two terms in office.

By December 1787, three states had ratified the Constitution and two more were about to do so. And all this without any substantial opposition in the conventions called to ratify the proposed Constitution, except for the Pennsylvania Minority Report (Document 15). But Jefferson's concerns about the absence of a bill of rights was a prominent theme in the pamphlet literature in fall 1787 (Documents 11, 13 and 14).

In December 1787, Madison was focused on securing rights by way of a fundamental alteration in the structure of the continental government rather than by imposing what he called "parchment barriers" on that government. He was also determined to save the proposed Constitution from the uncertainties of a second convention.

SOURCE: To James Madison from Thomas Jefferson, 27 December 1787 (*Founders Online*), https://goo.gl/ZaJfSg. For ease of reading, we have added paragraph divisions.

... The season admitting only of operations in the cabinet, and these being in great measure secret, I have little to fill a letter.[1] I will therefore make up

---

[1] Jefferson refers to the Court of Louis XVI.

the deficiency by adding a few words on the Constitution proposed by our Convention. I like much the general idea of framing a government which should go on itself peaceably, without needing continual recurrence to the state legislatures. I like the organization of the government into Legislative, Judiciary and Executive. I like the power given the legislature to levy taxes, and for that reason solely approve of the greater house being chosen by the people directly. For though I think a house chosen by them will be very ill qualified to legislate for the Union, for foreign nations, etc. yet this evil does not weigh against the good of preserving inviolate the fundamental principle that the people are not to be taxed but by representatives chosen immediately by themselves. I am captivated by the compromise of the opposite claims of the great and little states, of the latter to equal, and the former to proportional influence. I am much pleased too with the substitution of the method of voting by persons, instead of that of voting by states: and I like the negative given to the Executive with a third of either house, though I should have liked it better had the Judiciary been associated for that purpose, or invested with a similar and separate power. There are other good things of less moment.

I will now add what I do not like.

First the omission of a bill of rights providing clearly and without the aid of sophisms for freedom of religion, freedom of the press, protection against standing armies, restriction against monopolies, the eternal and unremitting force of the habeas corpus law, and trials by jury in all matter of fact triable by the laws of the land and not by the law of Nations. To say, as Mr. Wilson[2] does that a bill of rights was not necessary because all is reserved in the case of the general government which is not given, while in the particular ones all is given which is not reserved might do for the audience to whom it was addressed, but is surely gratis dictum,[3] opposed by strong inferences from the body of the instrument, as well as from the omission of the clause of our present confederation which had declared that in express terms.[4] It was a hard conclusion to say because there has been no uniformity among the states as to the cases triable by jury, because some have been so incautious as to abandon this mode of trial, therefore the more prudent states shall be reduced to the same level of calamity. It would have been much more just

---

[2] See Document 10, also Document 18.
[3] A gratuitous statement, in this case for the reasons Jefferson immediately gave
[4] Article II of the Articles of Confederation states "each state retains its sovereignty, freedom and independence, and every power, jurisdiction and right, which is not by this confederation expressly delegated to the United States in Congress assembled."

and wise to have concluded the other way that as most of the states had judiciously preserved this palladium, those who had wandered should be brought back to it, and to have established general right instead of general wrong. Let me add that a bill of rights is what the people are entitled to against every government on earth, general or particular, and what no just government should refuse, or rest on inference.

The second feature I dislike, and greatly dislike, is the abandonment in every instance of the necessity of rotation in office, and most particularly in the case of the President. Experience concurs with reason in concluding that the first magistrate will always be re-elected if the Constitution permits it. He is then an officer for life. This once observed it becomes of so much consequence to certain nations to have a friend or a foe at the head of our affairs that they will interfere with money and with arms....

Smaller objections are the appeal in fact as well as law, and the binding all persons Legislative, Executive and Judiciary by oath to maintain that constitution.

I do not pretend to decide what would be the best method of procuring the establishment of the manifold good things in this constitution, and of getting rid of the bad. Whether by adopting it in hopes of future amendment, or, after it has been duly weighted and canvassed by the people, after seeing the parts they generally dislike, and those they generally approve, to say to them "We see now what you wish. Send together your deputies again, let them frame a constitution for you omitting what you have condemned, and establishing the powers you approve. Even these will be a great addition to the energy of your government."

At all events I hope you will not be discouraged from other trials, if the present one should fail of its full effect....

Virginia Ratifying Convention

June 24–27, 1788

N ew Hampshire was the ninth state to ratify (57–47), thus ensuring ratification of the Constitution. Nevertheless, the delegates in Virginia and New York continued the conversation, in part, because they did not know in the early stages that New Hampshire had ratified.

The vote entering the Virginia Ratifying Convention was 84–84. The final vote was 89–79. Five delegates changed their minds because of a promise to consider alterations in the First Congress. The compromise thus reached represents the first time since the Pennsylvania Minority Report (Document 15) that a clear distinction was made between supporting or opposing structural amendments to the proposed Constitution and friendly amendments to include a bill of rights to restrain the powers of Congress. Amendments did not mean support for, or rejection of, a bill of rights. And support for a bill of rights did not mean that one supported structural amendments to the Constitution. That the U.S. Bill of Rights appeared as ten amendments to the original Constitution is the result of the politics of the First Congress (Documents 22–26).

James Madison vigorously opposed conditional ratification or calling a second Constitutional Convention. In the end, he voted in favor of adoption of the Constitution with "recommended" alterations to be considered in the First Congress. Representative Madison chose to follow the friendly bill of rights route rather than the unfriendly structural amendment route in the First Congress, even though in June 1787 he still considered a bill of rights to be unnecessary and dangerous.

SOURCE: The Debates in the Several State Conventions on the Adoption of the Federal Constitution … 2d ed., with considerable additions. Collected and rev. from contemporary publications, by Jonathan Elliot. Published under the sanction of Congress, 1836, 5 vols. These excerpts are from volume 3, pages 586, 588, 616–617, 662–663; https://goo.gl/JKrMq6. Text in brackets not italicized is from Elliot's volume. Italicized text in brackets is ours.

Tuesday, June 24, 1788

Mr. Wythe:[1]... recurred to the system under consideration [the Articles of Confederation]. He admitted its imperfection, and the propriety of some amendments. But the excellency of many parts of it could not be denied by its warmest opponents. He thought that experience was the best guide, and could alone develop its consequences. Most of the improvements that had been made in the science of government, and other sciences, were the result of experience....

...It appeared to him, most clearly, that any amendments which might be thought necessary would be easily obtained after ratification, in the manner proposed by the Constitution, as amendments were desired by all the states, and had already been proposed by the several states. He then proposed that the committee should ratify the Constitution, and that whatsoever amendments might be deemed necessary should be recommended to the consideration of the Congress which should first assemble under the Constitution, to be acted upon according to the mode prescribed therein.

The resolution of ratification proposed by Mr. Wythe was then read by the clerk.[2]

Whereas the powers granted under the proposed Constitution are the gift of the people, and every power not granted thereby remains with them, and at their will, no right, therefore, of any denomination, can be cancelled, abridged, restrained, or modified, by the Congress, by the Senate or House of Representatives, acting in any capacity, by the President, or any department or officer of the United States, except in those instances in which power is given by the Constitution for those purposes; and, among other essential rights, liberty of conscience and of the press cannot be cancelled, abridged, restrained, or modified, by any authority of the United States.

---

[1] George Wythe (1726–1806) was a law professor who was a teacher and mentor to Thomas Jefferson, John Marshall, and Henry Clay. As one of Virginia's representatives, he signed the Declaration of Independence and served in the Continental Congress and at the Constitutional Convention.

[2] We have inserted the resolution at this point in the text. In Eliott's volume it was printed under the proceedings for June 25, 1788.

Mr. HENRY,[3] after observing that the proposal of ratification was premature, and that the importance of the subject required the most mature deliberation, proceeded thus:

The honorable member must forgive me for declaring my dissent from it [the resolution proposed by Wythe]; because, if I understand it rightly, it admits that the new system is defective, and most capitally; for, immediately after the proposed ratification, there comes a declaration that the paper before you is not intended to violate any of these three great rights—the liberty of religion, liberty of the press, and the trial by jury. What is the inference when you enumerate the rights which you are to enjoy? That those not enumerated are relinquished. There are only three things to be retained—religion, freedom of the press, and jury trial. Will not the ratification carry everything, without excepting these three things? Will not all the world pronounce that we intended to give up all the rest? Everything it speaks of, by way of rights, is comprised in these things. Your subsequent amendments only go to these three amendments...

[Here Mr. Henry informed the committee that he had a resolution prepared, to refer a declaration of rights, with certain amendments to the most exceptionable parts of the Constitution, to the other states in the confederacy, for their consideration, previous to its ratification. The clerk then read the resolution, the declaration of rights, and amendments....][4]

[Proposed Bill of Rights]

That there be a declaration or bill of rights asserting, and securing from encroachment, the essential and unalienable rights of the people, in some such manner as the following:

1st. That there are certain natural rights, of which men, when they form a social compact, cannot deprive or divest their posterity; among which are the enjoyment of life and liberty, with the means of acquiring, possessing, and protecting property, and pursuing and obtaining happiness and safety.

---

[3] Patrick Henry (1736–1799) was a lawyer and politician who served in the Continental Congress and twice as Governor of Virginia.
[4] We have inserted the proposed Bill of Rights and the amendments at this point in the text. In Eliott's volume they were printed under the proceedings for June 27, 1788.

2d. That all power is naturally invested in, and consequently derived from, the people; that magistrates therefore are their trustees and agents, at all times amenable to them.

3d. That government ought to be instituted for the common benefit, protection, and security of the people; and that the doctrine of non-resistance against arbitrary power and oppression is absurd, slavish, and destructive to the good and happiness of mankind.

4th. That no man or set of men are entitled to separate or exclusive public emoluments or privileges from the community, but in consideration of public services, which not being descendible, neither ought the offices of magistrate, legislator, or judge, or any other public office, to be hereditary.

5th. That the legislative, executive, and judicial powers of government should be separate and distinct; and, that the members of the two first may be restrained from oppression by feeling and participating the public burdens, they should, at fixed periods, be reduced to a private station, return into the mass of the people, and the vacancies be supplied by certain and regular elections, in which all or any part of the former members to be eligible or ineligible, as the rules of the Constitution of government, and the laws, shall direct.

6th. That the elections of representatives in the legislature ought to be free and frequent, and all men having sufficient evidence of permanent common interest with, and attachment to, the community, ought to have the right of suffrage; and no aid, charge, tax, or fee, can be set, rated, or levied, upon the people without their own consent, or that of their representatives, so elected; nor can they be bound by any law to which they have not, in like manner, assented, for the public good.

7th. That all power of suspending laws, or the execution of laws, by any authority, without the consent of the representatives of the people in the legislature, is injurious to their rights, and ought not to be exercised.

8th. That, in all criminal and capital prosecutions, a man hath a right to demand the cause and nature of his accusation, to be confronted with the accusers and witnesses, to call for evidence, and be allowed counsel in his favor, and to a fair and speedy trial by an impartial jury of his vicinage, without whose unanimous consent he cannot be found guilty, (except in the government of the land and naval forces;) nor can he be compelled to give evidence against himself.

9th. That no freeman ought to be taken, imprisoned, or disseized[5] of his freehold, liberties, privileges, or franchises, or outlawed, or exiled, or in any manner destroyed, or deprived of his life, liberty, or property, but by the law of the land.

10th. That every freeman restrained of his liberty is entitled to a remedy, to inquire into the lawfulness thereof, and to remove the same, if unlawful, and that such remedy ought not to be denied nor delayed.

11th. That, in controversies respecting property, and in suits between man and man, the ancient trial by jury is one of the greatest securities to the rights of the people, and to remain sacred and inviolable.

12th. That every freeman ought to find a certain remedy, by recourse to the laws, for all injuries and wrongs he may receive in his person, property, or character. He ought to obtain right and justice freely, without sale, completely and without denial, promptly and without delay; and that all establishments or regulations contravening these rights are oppressive and unjust.

13th. That excessive bail ought not to be required, nor excessive fines imposed, nor cruel and unusual punishments inflicted.

14th. That every freeman has a right to be secure from all unreasonable searches and seizures of his person, his papers, and property; all warrants, therefore, to search suspected places, or seize any freeman, his papers, or property, without information on oath (or affirmation of a person religiously scrupulous of taking an oath) of legal and sufficient cause, are grievous and oppressive; and all general warrants to search suspected places, or to apprehend any suspected person, without specially naming or describing the place or person, are dangerous, and ought not to be granted.

15th. That the people have a right peaceably to assemble together.

16th. That the people have a right to freedom of speech, and of writing and publishing their sentiments; that the freedom of the press is one of the greatest bulwarks of liberty, and ought not to be violated.

17th. That the people have a right to keep and bear arms; that a well-regulated militia, composed of the body of the people trained

---

[5] deprived

to arms, is the proper, natural, and safe defense of a free state; that standing armies, in time of peace, are dangerous to liberty, and therefore ought to be avoided, as far as the circumstances and protection of the community will admit; and that, in all cases, the military should be under strict subordination to, and governed by, the civil power.

18th. That no soldier in time of peace ought to be quartered in any house without the consent of the owner, and in time of war in such manner only as the law directs.

19th. That any person religiously scrupulous of bearing arms ought to be exempted, upon payment of an equivalent to employ another to bear arms in his stead.

20th. That religion, or the duty which we owe to our Creator, and the manner of discharging it, can be directed only by reason and conviction, not by force or violence; and therefore all men have an equal, natural, and unalienable right to the free exercise of religion, according to the dictates of conscience, and that no particular religious sect or society ought to be favored or established, by law, in preference to others.

[PROPOSED] Amendments to the Constitution

1st. That each state in the Union shall respectively retain every power, jurisdiction, and right, which is not by this Constitution delegated to the Congress of the United States, or to the departments of the federal government.

2d. That there shall be one representative for every thirty thousand, according to the enumeration or census mentioned in the Constitution, until the whole number of representatives amounts to two hundred; after which, that number shall be continued or increased, as Congress shall direct, upon the principles fixed in the Constitution, by apportioning the representatives of each state to some greater number of people, from time to time, as population increases.

3d. When the Congress shall lay direct taxes or excises, they shall immediately inform the executive power of each state, of the quota of such state, according to the census herein directed, which is proposed to be thereby raised; and if the legislature of any state shall pass a law which shall be effectual for raising such quota at the time required by Congress, the taxes and excises laid by Congress shall not be collected in such state.

4th.   That the members of the Senate and House of Representatives shall be ineligible to, and incapable of holding, any civil office under the authority of the United States, during the time for which they shall respectively be elected.

5th.   That the journals of the proceedings of the Senate and House of Representatives shall be published at least once in every year. except such parts thereof, relating to treaties, alliances, or military operations, as, in their judgment, require secrecy.

6th.   That a regular statement and account of the receipts and expenditures of public money shall be published at least once a year.

7th.   That no commercial treaty shall be ratified without the concurrence of two thirds of the whole number of the members of the Senate; and no treaty ceding, contracting, restraining, or suspending, the territorial rights or claims of the United States, or any of them, or their, or any of their rights or claims to fishing in the American seas, or navigating the American rivers, shall be made, but in cases of the most urgent and extreme necessity; nor shall any such treaty be ratified without the concurrence of three fourths of the whole number of the members of both houses respectively.

8th.   That no navigation law, or law regulating commerce, shall be passed without the consent of two thirds of the members present, in both houses.

9th.   That no standing army, or regular troops, shall be raised, or kept up, in time of peace, without the consent of two thirds of the members present, in both houses.

10th.   That no soldier shall be enlisted for any longer term than four years, except in time of war, and then for no longer term than the continuance of the war.

11th.   That each state respectively shall have the power to provide for organizing, arming, and disciplining its own militia, when so ever Congress shall omit or neglect to provide for the same. That the militia shall not be subject to martial law, except when in actual service, in time of war, invasion, or rebellion; and when not in the actual service of the United States, shall be subject only to such fines, penalties, and punishments, as shall be directed or inflicted by the laws of its own state.

12th. That the exclusive power of legislation given to Congress over the federal town and its adjacent district, and other places, purchased or to be purchased by Congress of any of the states, shall extend only to such regulations as respect the police and good government thereof.

13th. That no person shall be capable of being President of the United States for more than eight years in any term of sixteen years.

14th. That the judicial power of the United States shall be vested in one Supreme Court, and in such courts of admiralty as Congress may from time to time ordain and establish in any of the different states. The judicial power shall extend to all cases in law and equity arising under treaties made, or which shall be made, under the authority of the United States; to all cases affecting ambassadors, other foreign ministers, and consuls; to all cases of admiralty and maritime jurisdiction; to controversies to which the United States shall be a party; to controversies between two or more states, and between parties claiming lands under the grants of different states. In all cases affecting ambassadors, other foreign ministers, and consuls, and those in which a state shall be a party, the Supreme Court shall have original jurisdiction; in all other cases before mentioned, the Supreme Court shall have appellate jurisdiction, as to matters of law only, except in cases of equity, and of admiralty, and maritime jurisdiction, in which the Supreme Court shall have appellate jurisdiction both as to law and fact, with such exceptions and under such regulations as the Congress shall make: but the judicial power of the United States shall extend to no case where the cause of action shall have originated before the ratification of the Constitution, except in disputes between states about their territory, disputes between persons claiming lands under, the grants of different states, and suits for debts due to the United States.

15th. That, in criminal prosecutions, no man shall be restrained in the exercise of the usual and accustomed right of challenging or excepting to the jury.

16th. That Congress shall not alter, modify, or interfere in the times, places, or manner of holding elections for senators and representatives, or either of them, except when the legislature of any state shall neglect, refuse, or be disabled, by invasion or rebellion, to prescribe the same.

17th. That those clauses which declare that Congress shall not exercise certain powers, be not interpreted, in any manner whatsoever, to extend the powers of Congress; but that they be construed either as making exceptions to the specified powers where this shall be the case, or otherwise, as inserted merely for greater caution.

18th. That the laws ascertaining the compensation of senators and representatives for their services, be postponed, in their operation, until after the election of representatives immediately Succeeding the passing thereof; that excepted which shall first be passed on the subject.

19th. That some tribunal other than the Senate be provided for trying impeachments of senators.

20th. That the salary of a judge shall not be increased or diminished during his continuance in office, otherwise than by general regulations of salary, which may take place on a revision of the subject at stated periods of not less than seven years, to commence from the time such salaries shall be first ascertained by Congress.

[At this point, Henry reminded the delegates that what the citizens of Virginia wanted was to "be able to sit down in peace and security under their own fig-trees."[6] Edmund Randolph suggested that Henry was advocating that Virginia secede if the Constitution was adopted without "previous amendments." Henry denied having said anything of secession. Randolph responded, is it not a secession from the principles of republican government, and "good citizenship" when a minority refuses to "submit to the decision of the majority."]

... Mr. Madison: nothing has excited more admiration in the world than the manner in which free governments have been established in America; for it was the first instance, from the creation of the world to the American revolution, that free inhabitants have been seen deliberating on a form of government, and selecting such of their citizens as possessed their confidence, to determine upon and give effect to it. ...

... Mr. Madison conceived that what defects might be in the Constitution might be removed by the amendatory mode in itself. As to a solemn declaration of our essential rights, he thought it unnecessary and dangerous:

---

[6] Micah 4:4, one of the most popular and often quoted Biblical passages during the Revolution and the years following. For example, George Washington quoted it in his Letter to the Hebrew Congregation in Newport, August 21, 1790.

unnecessary, because it was evident that the general government had no power but what was given it, and that the delegation alone warranted the exercise of power; dangerous, because an enumeration which is not complete is not safe.... He declared that such amendments as seemed, in his judgment, to be without danger, he would readily admit, and that he would be the last to oppose any such amendment as would give satisfaction to any gentleman, unless it were dangerous.

Wednesday, June 25, 1788

[Madison believed that introducing amendments to the Constitution prior to ratifying it would send a confused message to the states that have already ratified and cause "unnecessary delays." Amendments should be made through the process defined in the Constitution. James Monroe considered it to be more prudent to secure previous (and binding) amendments than subsequent (and recommendatory) amendments. Henry argued that "the proposition of subsequent amendments is only to lull our apprehensions." Randolph repeated his point that with ratification by eight states, Virginia's deliberations had become "the single question of Union or no Union." The need to preserve the Union persuaded Randolph to now ratify the proposed constitution, although he had opposed it at the Constitutional Convention.]

The clerk then read the revision of Wythe's earlier resolution:

Whereas the powers granted under the proposed Constitution are the gift of the people, and every power not granted thereby remains with them, and at their will,—no right, therefore, of any denomination, can be cancelled, abridged, restrained, or modified, by the Congress, by the Senate or House of Representatives, acting in any capacity, by the President, or any department or officer of the United States, except in those instances in which power is given by the Constitution for those purposes; and, among other essential rights, liberty of conscience and of the press cannot be cancelled, abridged, restrained, or modified, by any authority of the United States.

And whereas any imperfections, which may exist in the said Constitution, ought rather to be examined in the mode prescribed therein for obtaining amendments, than by a delay, with a hope of obtaining previous amendments, to bring the Union into danger.

Resolved, That it is the opinion of this committee, that the said Constitution be ratified. But in order to relieve the apprehensions of those who may be solicitous for amendments,–

Resolved, That it is the opinion of this committee, that whatsoever

amendments may be deemed necessary, be recommended to the consideration of the Congress which shall first assemble under the said Constitution,
to be acted upon according to the mode prescribed in the 5th article thereof."

The 1st resolution [that the Constitution be ratified] being read a second
time, a motion was made, and the question being put, to amend the same
by substituting, in lieu of the said resolution and its preamble, the following
resolution,–

Resolved, That, previous to the ratification of the new Constitution of
government recommended by the late federal Convention, a declaration of
rights, asserting, and securing from encroachment, the great principles of
civil and religious liberty, and the unalienable rights of the people, together
with amendments to the most exceptionable parts of the said Constitution
of government, ought to be referred by this Convention to the other states
in the American confederacy for their consideration.

It passed in the negative: ayes, 80; noes, 88. . . .

And then, the main question being put that the Convention do *agree* with
the committee in the said 1st resolution [that the constitution be ratified], it
was resolved in the affirmative—ayes, 89; noes, 79. . . .

Friday, June 27, 1788

. . . Mr. WYTHE reported, from the committee appointed, such amendments
to the proposed Constitution of government for the United States [those
listed above in this document] as were by them deemed necessary to be recommended to the consideration of the Congress which shall first assemble
under the said Constitution, to be acted upon according to the mode prescribed in the 5th article thereof . . . [7]

. . . [T]he main question being put, that this Convention doth concur with
the committee in the said amendments,—

It was resolved in the affirmative.

---

[7] Article V prescribes how the Constitution may be amended.

New York Ratifying Convention

June 17–July 25, 1788

New York followed Virginia's example (Document 17) of distinguishing between amendments that went to the heart of the proposed Constitution on the one hand, and on the other, a bill of rights that would be a "civic education" reminder to the people concerning what was at stake, as well as a constraint on the abuse of power by elected or appointed officials.

The delegates made their way through the Constitution from start to finish. Next came the big question. Should the Constitution be ratified "conditionally" on the adoption of proposals for amendments and a bill of rights or with "full confidence" that the First Congress would actively pursue the adoption of amendments and a bill of rights? John Lansing and Abraham Yates—New York delegates who attended and left the Philadelphia Convention halfway through—and Governor George Clinton supported conditional ratification, going so far as to suggest that if these conditions were not met in the First Congress, then New York should consider seceding from the union. They were particularly interested in the adoption of the thirty-one amendment proposals that directly confronted the work of the Framers. Alexander Hamilton, and the prominent Antifederalist politician and writer Melancton Smith, supported the "full confidence" approach with particular emphasis on the adoption of a bill of rights. Going into the Convention, John Lansing and Robert Yates had the votes to reject the Constitution: 46–19. The Constitution was adopted however, without conditions, on July 25 by a vote of 30–27. Smith, who may have had a hand in the Federal Farmer essays, as well as authoring the Brutus essays, persuaded more than ten Antifederalists to vote in favor of adopting the Constitution with the expectation that the First Congress would revisit the issue of Amendments and a Bill of Rights. Besides, argued Smith, the Constitution had already been adopted by ten states. Wasn't it better to accept adoption and seek relief in the First Congress than make a petulant statement? Eight delegates, including Governor Clinton, the presumed author of the Antifederalist Cato essays, abstained.

SOURCE: The Debates in the several State Conventions on the Adoption of the Federal Constitution, as Recommended by the General Convention at Philadelphia in 1787, 2d ed., with considerable additions. Collected and rev. from contemporary publications, by Jonathan Elliot. Published under the sanction of Congress. (1836), 5 vols.; https://goo.gl/yRg4Q7.

Bill of Rights

We the delegates of the people of the State of New York, duly elected and met in convention, having maturely considered the Constitution for the United States of America, agreed to on the seventeenth day of September, in the year one thousand seven hundred and eighty-seven, by the Convention then assembled at Philadelphia in the Commonwealth of Pennsylvania (a copy whereof precedes these presents) and having also seriously and deliberately considered the present situation of the United States, do declare and make known.

That all power is originally vested in and consequently derived from the people, and that government is instituted by them for their common Interest protection and security.

That the enjoyment of life, liberty and the pursuit of happiness are essential rights which every government ought to respect and preserve.

That the powers of government may be reassumed by the people, when so ever it shall become necessary to their happiness; that every power, jurisdiction and right, which is not by the said Constitution clearly delegated to the Congress of the United States, or the departments of the government thereof, remains to the people of the several states, or to their respective state governments to whom they may have granted the same. And that those clauses in the said Constitution, which declare, that Congress shall not have or exercise certain powers, do not imply that Congress is entitled to any powers not given by the said Constitution; but such clauses are to be construed either as exceptions to certain specified powers, or as inserted merely for greater caution.

That the people have an equal, natural and unalienable right, freely and peaceably to exercise their religion according to the dictates of conscience, and that no religious sect or society ought to be favored or established by law in preference of others.

That the people have a right to keep and bear arms; that a well regulated militia, including the body of the people capable of bearing arms is the proper, natural and safe defense of a free state.

That the militia should not be subject to martial law except in time of war, rebellion or insurrection.

That standing armies in time of peace are dangerous to liberty, and ought not to be kept up, except in cases of necessity; and that at all times, the military should be under strict subordination to the civil power.

That in time of peace no soldier ought to be quartered in any house without the consent of the owner, and in time of war only by the civil magistrate in such manner as the laws may direct.

That no person ought to be taken imprisoned or disseized[1] of his freehold, or be exiled or deprived of his privileges, franchises, life, liberty or property but by due process of law.

That no person ought to be put twice in jeopardy of life or limb for one and the same offence, nor, unless in case of impeachment, be punished more than once for the same offence.

That every person restrained of his liberty is entitled to an enquiry into the lawfulness of such restraint, and to a removal thereof if unlawful, and that such enquiry and removal ought not to be denied or delayed, except when on account of public danger the congress shall suspend the privilege of the writ of habeas corpus.

That excessive bail ought not to be required; nor excessive fines imposed; nor cruel or unusual punishments inflicted.

That (except in the government of the land and naval forces, and of the militia when in actual service, and in cases of impeachment) a presentment or indictment by a grand jury ought to be observed as a necessary preliminary to the trial of all crimes cognizable by the judiciary of the United States, and such trial should be speedy, public, and by an impartial jury of the county where the crime was committed; and that no person can be found guilty without the unanimous consent of such jury. But in cases of crimes not committed within any county of any of the United States, and in cases of crimes committed within any county in which a general Insurrection may prevail, or which may be in the possession of a foreign enemy, the enquiry and trial may be in such county as the Congress shall by law direct; which county in the two cases last mentioned should be as near as conveniently may be to that county in which the crime may have been committed.

And that in all criminal prosecutions, the accused ought to be informed of the cause and nature of his accusation, to be confronted with his accusers and the witnesses against him, to have the means of producing his witnesses, and the assistance of counsel for his defense, and should not be compelled to give evidence against himself.

---

[1] deprived

That the trial by jury in the extent that it obtains by the common law of England is one of the greatest securities to the rights of a free people, and ought to remain inviolate.

That every freeman has a right to be secure from all unreasonable searches and seizures of his person his papers or his property, and therefore, that all warrants to search suspected places or seize any freeman his papers or property, without information upon oath or affirmation of sufficient cause, are grievous and oppressive; and that all general warrants (or such in which the place or person suspected are not particularly designated) are dangerous and ought not to be granted.

That the people have a right peaceably to assemble together to consult for their common good, or to instruct their Representatives; and that every person has a right to petition or apply to the legislature for redress of grievances.

That the freedom of the press ought not to be violated or restrained.

That there should be once in four years an election of the President and Vice President, so that no officer who may be appointed by the Congress to act as President in case of the removal, death, resignation or inability of the President and Vice President can in any case continue to act beyond the termination of the period for which the last President and Vice President were elected.

That nothing contained in the said Constitution is to be construed to prevent the legislature of any state from passing laws at its discretion from time to time to divide such state into convenient districts, and to apportion its Representatives to and amongst such districts.

That the prohibition contained in the said Constitution against ex post facto laws, extends only to laws concerning crimes.

That all appeals in causes determinable according to the course of the common law, ought to be by writ of error[2] and not otherwise.

That the judicial power of the United States in cases in which a state may be a party, does not extend to criminal prosecutions, or to authorize any suit by any person against a state.

That the judicial power of the United States as to controversies between citizens of the same state claiming lands under grants of different states is not to be construed to extend to any other controversies between them except those which relate to such lands, so claimed under grants of different states.

---

[2] A writ from a Court of Appeals to the court that heard the case under appeal requiring that the court send the trial record to the Court of Appeals

That the jurisdiction of the Supreme Court of the United States, or of any other court to be instituted by the Congress, is not in any case to be increased enlarged or extended by any fiction, collusion, or mere suggestion. And that no treaty is to be construed so to operate as to alter the constitution of any state.

Under these impressions and declaring that the rights aforesaid cannot be abridged or violated, and that the explanations aforesaid are consistent with the said Constitution, and in confidence that the amendments which shall have been proposed to the said Constitution will receive an early and mature consideration: We the said delegates, in the name and in the behalf of the people of the State of New York do by these presents assent to and ratify the said Constitution. In full confidence nevertheless that until a convention shall be called and convened for proposing amendments to the said Constitution, the militia of this state will not be continued in service out of this state for a longer term than six weeks without the consent of the legislature thereof; that the Congress will not make or alter any regulation in this state respecting the times places and manner of holding elections for Senators or Representatives unless the legislature of this state shall neglect or refuse to make laws or regulations for the purpose, or from any circumstance be incapable of making the same, and that in those cases such power will only be exercised until the legislature of this state shall make provision in the premises; that no excise[3] will be imposed on any article of the growth, production, or manufacture of the United States, or any of them within this state, ardent spirits excepted; and that the Congress will not lay direct taxes[4] within this state, but when the monies arising from the impost[5] and excise shall be insufficient for the public exigencies, nor then, until Congress shall first have made a requisition upon this state to assess levy and pay the amount of such requisition made agreeably to the census fixed in the said Constitution in such way and manner as the legislature of this state shall judge best, but that in such case, if the state shall neglect or refuse to pay its proportion pursuant to such requisition, then the Congress may assess and levy this state's proportion together with interest at the rate of six per centum per annum from the time at which the same was required to be paid.

Done in convention at Poughkeepsie in the County of Dutchess in the

---

[3] a tax on goods bought or sold within a country
[4] a tax on individuals
[5] a tax on items imported

State of New York the twenty sixth day of July in the year of our Lord one thousand seven hundred and eighty-eight.

By Order of the Convention.
Geo: Clinton president
Attested

John McKesson
Abm. B. Bancker
Secretaries

Amendments

AND the Convention do in the name and behalf of the people of the State of New York enjoin it upon their Representatives in the Congress, to exert all their Influence, and use all reasonable means to obtain a ratification of the following amendments to the said Constitution in the manner prescribed therein; and in all laws to be passed by the Congress in the meantime to conform to the spirit of the said amendments as far as the Constitution will admit.

That there shall be one Representative for every thirty thousand Inhabitants, according to the enumeration or census mentioned in the Constitution, until the whole number of Representatives amounts to two hundred; after which that number shall be continued or increased but not diminished, as Congress shall direct, and according to such ratio as the Congress shall fix, in conformity to the rule prescribed for the apportionment of Representatives and direct taxes.

That the Congress do not impose any excise on any article (except ardent spirits) of the growth, production, or manufacture of the United States, or any of them.

That Congress do not lay direct taxes but when the monies arising from the impost and excise shall be insufficient for the public exigencies, nor then until Congress shall first have made a requisition upon the states to assess levy and pay their respective proportions of such requisition, agreeably to the census fixed in the said Constitution, in such way and manner as the legislatures of the respective states shall judge best; and in such case, if any state shall neglect or refuse to pay its proportion pursuant to such requisition, then Congress may assess and levy such states proportion, together with interest at the rate of six per centum per annum, from the time of payment prescribed in such requisition.

That the Congress shall not make or alter any regulation in any state respecting the times places and manner of holding elections for Senators or Representatives, unless the legislature of such state shall neglect or refuse to make laws or regulations for the purpose, or from any circumstance be incapable of making the same; and then only until the legislature of such state shall make provision in the premises; provided that Congress may prescribe the time for the election of Representatives.

That no persons except natural born citizens, or such as were citizens on or before the fourth day of July one thousand seven hundred and seventy-six, or such as held commissions under the United States during the war, and have at any time since the fourth day of July one thousand seven hundred and seventy six become citizens of one or other of the United States, and who shall be freeholders, shall be eligible to the places of President, Vice President, or members of either House of the Congress of the United States.

That the Congress do not grant monopolies or erect any company with exclusive advantages of commerce.

That no standing army or regular troops shall be raised or kept up in time of peace, without the consent of two-thirds of the Senators and Representatives present, in each House.

That no money be borrowed on the credit of the United States without the assent of two-thirds of the Senators and Representatives present in each House.

That the Congress shall not declare war without the concurrence of two-thirds of the Senators and Representatives present in each House.

That the privilege of the habeas corpus shall not by any law be suspended for a longer term than six months, or until twenty days after the meeting of the Congress next following the passing of the act for such suspension.

That the right of the Congress to exercise exclusive legislation over such district, not exceeding ten miles square, as may by cession of a particular state, and the acceptance of Congress, become the seat of the government of the United States, shall not be so exercised, as to exempt the inhabitants of such district from paying the like taxes, imposts, duties,[6] and excises, as shall be imposed on the other inhabitants of the state in which such district may be; and that no person shall be privileged within the said district from arrest for crimes committed or debts contracted out of the said district.

That the right of exclusive legislation with respect to such places as may be purchased for the erection of forts, magazines, arsenals, dockyards and

---

[6] a tax on imported goods

other needful buildings shall not authorize the Congress to make any law to prevent the laws of the states respectively in which they may be from extending to such places in all civil and criminal matters except as to such persons as shall be in the service of the United States; nor to them with respect to crimes committed without such places.

That the compensation for the Senators and Representatives be ascertained by standing laws; and that no alteration of the existing rate of compensation shall operate for the benefit of the Representatives, until after a subsequent election shall have been had.

That the journals of the Congress shall be published at least once a year, with the exception of such parts relating to treaties or military operations, as in the judgment of either House shall require secrecy; and that both Houses of Congress shall always keep their doors open during their sessions, unless the business may in their opinion require secrecy. That the yeas & nays shall be entered on the journals whenever two members in either House may require it.

That no capitation tax[7] shall ever be laid by the Congress.

That no person be eligible as a Senator for more than six years in any term of twelve years; and that the legislatures of the respective states may recall their Senators or either of them, and elect others in their stead, to serve the remainder of the time for which the Senators so recalled were appointed.

That no Senator or Representative shall during the time for which he was elected be appointed to any office under the authority of the United States.

That the authority given to the Executives of the States to fill the vacancies of Senators be abolished, and that such vacancies be filled by the respective legislatures.

That the power of Congress to pass uniform laws concerning bankruptcy shall only extend to merchants and other traders; and that the states respectively may pass laws for the relief of other insolvent debtors.

That no person shall be eligible to the office of President of the United States a third time.

That the Executive shall not grant pardons for treason, unless with the consent of the Congress; but may at his discretion grant reprieves[8] to persons convicted of treason, until their cases, can be laid before the Congress.

That the President or person exercising his powers for the time being,

---

[7] a tax on an individual at a fixed rate
[8] cancel or delay punishment

shall not command an army in the field in person, without the previous desire of the Congress.

That all letters patent,[9] commissions, pardons, writs,[10] and process of the United States, shall run in the name of the people of the United States, and be tested in the name of the President of the United States, or the person exercising his powers for the time being, or the first judge of the court out of which the same shall issue, as the case may be.

That the Congress shall not constitute ordain or establish any tribunals or inferior courts, with any other than appellate jurisdiction, except such as may be necessary for the trial of causes of admiralty and maritime jurisdiction, and for the trial of piracies and felonies committed on the high seas; and in all other cases to which the judicial power of the United States extends, and in which the Supreme Court of the United States has not original jurisdiction, the causes shall be heard, tried, and determined in some one of the State courts, with the right of appeal to the Supreme Court of the United States, or other proper tribunal to be established for that purpose by the Congress, with such exceptions, and under such regulations as the Congress shall make.

That the court for the trial of impeachments shall consist of the Senate, the judges of the Supreme Court of the United States, and the first or senior judge for the time being, of the highest court of general and ordinary common law jurisdiction in each State; that the Congress shall by standing laws designate the courts in the respective states answering this description, and in states having no courts exactly answering this description, shall designate some other court, preferring such if any there be, whose judge or judges may hold their places during good behavior.

Provided that no more than one judge, other than judges of the Supreme Court of the United States, shall come from one state. That the Congress be authorized to pass laws for compensating the said judges for such services and for compelling their attendance and that a majority at least of the said judges shall be requisite to constitute the said court. That no person impeached shall sit as a member thereof. That each member shall previous to the entering upon any trial take an oath or affirmation, honestly and impartially to hear and determine the cause and that a majority of the members present shall be necessary to a conviction.

That persons aggrieved by any judgment, sentence or decree of the

---

[9] a patent or legal monopoly over an invention
[10] written order issued by a court

Supreme Court of the United States, in any cause in which that court has original jurisdiction, with such exceptions, and under such regulations, as the Congress shall make concerning the same, shall, upon application, have a commission to be issued by the President of the United States, to such men learned in the law as he shall nominate, and by and with the advice and consent of the Senate appoint, not less than seven, authorizing such commissioners, or any seven or more of them, to correct the errors in such judgment or to review such sentence and decree, as the case may be, and to do justice to the parties in the premises.

That no judge of the Supreme Court of the United States shall hold any other office under the United States, or any of them.

That the judicial power of the United States shall extend to no controversies respecting land, unless it relate to claims of territory or jurisdiction between states, or to claims of land between individuals, or between states and individuals under the grants of different states.

That the militia of any state shall not be compelled to serve without the limits of the state for a longer term than six weeks, without the consent of the legislature thereof.

That the words "without the consent of the Congress" in the seventh clause of the ninth section of the first article of the Constitution, be expunged.[11]

That the Senators and Representatives and all executive and judicial officers of the United States shall be bound by oath or affirmation not to infringe or violate the Constitutions or rights of the respective states.

That the legislatures of the respective states may make provision by law, that the electors of the election districts to be by them appointed shall choose a citizen of the United States who shall have been an inhabitant of such district for the term of one year immediately preceding the time of his election, for one of the Representatives of such State.

Done in convention at Poughkeepsie in the county of Dutchess in the State of New York the twenty-sixth day of July in the year of our Lord one thousand seven hundred and eighty-eight.

---

[11] An apparent reference to the Article I, section 9 "No title of nobility shall be granted by the United States: And no person holding any office of profit and trust under them, shall, without the consent of the Congress, accept of any present, emolument, office, or title, of any kind whatever, from any king, prince, or foreign state."

Federalist 84

July 16, 1788

T his is the second longest essay in *The Federalist*, a collection of newspaper essays by Publius (Alexander Hamilton, James Madison and John Jay; Hamilton wrote number 84) published in New York City to support adoption of the Constitution. It summarizes Federalist arguments that the proposed Constitution does not need a bill of rights. The ratification campaign was basically over. The Constitution had been ratified and a promise to consider a bill of rights had been agreed to. Nevertheless, Publius refused to recognize this political reality and virtually repeated James Wilson's State House Speech made at the beginning of the campaign (Document 10). Wilson's speech and Federalist 84 provide bookends to the argument as to why a bill of rights is unnecessary and even dangerous. Madison in Virginia and Hamilton in New York (Documents 17, 18) agreed to the Constitution's adoption on the hope of a friendly revision of the Constitution in the First Congress.

SOURCE: *The Federalist: The Gideon Edition*, eds. George W. Carey and James McClellan (Indianapolis: Liberty Fund, 2001), 442–451.

IN THE course of the foregoing review of the Constitution, I have taken notice of, and endeavored to answer most of the objections which have appeared against it. There however remain a few which either did not fall naturally under any particular head or were forgotten in their proper places. These shall now be discussed; but as the subject has been drawn into great length, I shall so far consult brevity as to comprise all my observations on these miscellaneous points in a single paper.

The most considerable of the remaining objections is that the plan of the convention contains no bill of rights. Among other answers given to this, it has been upon different occasions remarked that the constitutions of several of the states are in a similar predicament. I add that New York is of the number. And yet the persons who in this state oppose the new system, while they profess an unlimited admiration for its constitution, are among the most intemperate partisans of a bill of rights. To justify their zeal in this matter they allege two things: one is that though the constitution of New York has no bill of rights prefixed to it, yet it contains, in the body of it, various provisions in favor of particular privileges and rights which, in substance, amount to the same thing; the other is that the Constitution adopts, in their full extent, the common and statute law of Great Britain, by which many other rights, not expressed, are equally secured.

To the first I answer that the Constitution proposed by the convention contains, as well as the constitution of this state, a number of such provisions.

Independent of those which relate to the structure of the government, we find the following: Article 1, section 3, clause 7—"Judgment in cases of impeachment shall not extend further than to removal from office and disqualification to hold and enjoy any office of honor, trust, or profit under the United States; but the party convicted shall nevertheless, be liable and subject to indictment, trial, judgment, and punishment according to law." Section 9, of the same article, clause 2—"The privilege of the writ of habeas corpus shall not be suspended, unless when in cases of rebellion or invasion the public safety may require it." Clause 3—"No bill of attainder or ex post facto law shall be passed." Clause 7—"No title of nobility shall be granted by the United States; and no person holding any office of profit or trust under them shall, without the consent of the Congress, accept of any present, emolument, office, or title of any kind whatever, from any king, prince, or foreign state." Article III, section 2, clause 3—"The trial of all crimes, except in cases of impeachment, shall be by jury; and such trial shall be held in the State where the said crimes shall have been committed; but when not committed within any State, the trial shall be at such place or places as the Congress may by law have directed." Section 3 of the same article—"Treason against the United States shall consist only in levying war against them, or in adhering to their enemies, giving them aid and comfort. No person shall be convicted of treason, unless on the testimony of two witnesses to the same overt act, or on confession in open court." And clause 3, of the same section—"The Congress shall have power to declare the punishment of treason; but no attainder of treason shall work corruption of blood, or forfeiture, except during the life of the person attainted."

It may well be a question whether these are not, upon the whole, of equal importance with any which are to be found in the constitution of this state. The establishment of the writ of habeas corpus, the prohibition of ex-post-facto laws, and of titles of nobility, to which we have no corresponding provision in our Constitution, are perhaps greater securities to

liberty and republicanism than any it contains. The creation of crimes after
the commission of the fact, or, in other words, the subjecting of men to punishment for things which, when they were done, were breaches of no law, and
the practice of arbitrary imprisonments, have been, in all ages, the favorite
and most formidable instruments of tyranny. The observations of the judicious Blackstone,[1] in reference to the latter, are well worthy of recital: "To
bereave a man of life [says he] or by violence to confiscate his estate, without
accusation or trial, would be so gross and notorious an act of despotism as
must at once convey the alarm of tyranny throughout the whole nation; but
confinement of the person, by secretly hurrying him to jail, where his suffer-
ings are unknown or forgotten, is a less public, a less striking, and therefore
a more dangerous engine of arbitrary government." And as a remedy for this
fatal evil he is everywhere peculiarly emphatical in his encomiums on the
habeas corpus act, which in one place he calls "the bulwark of the British
Constitution."

Nothing need be said to illustrate the importance of the prohibition of
titles of nobility. This may truly be denominated the cornerstone of republican government for so long as they are excluded there can never be serious
danger that the government will be any other than that of the people.

To the second, that is, to the pretended establishment of the common
and statute law by the Constitution, I answer that they are expressly made
subject "to such alterations and provisions as the legislature shall from time
to time make concerning the same." They are therefore at any moment liable
to repeal by the ordinary legislative power, and of course have no constitutional sanction. The only use of the declaration was to recognize the ancient
law and to remove doubts which might have been occasioned by the Revolution. This consequently can be considered as no part of a declaration of
rights, which under our constitutions must be intended as limitations of the
power of the government itself.

It has been several times truly remarked that bills of rights are, in their
origin, stipulations between kings and their subjects, abridgements of prerogative in favor of privilege, reservations of rights not surrendered to the
prince. Such was Magna Charta,[2] obtained by the barons, sword in hand,
from King John. Such were the subsequent confirmations of that charter by
subsequent princes. Such was the Petition of the Right assented to by Charles

---

[1] William Blackstone (1723–1780), an English jurist, wrote an influential commen-
tary on the laws of England.
[2] 1215

the First in the beginning of his reign. Such, also, was the Declaration of Right presented by the Lords and Commons to the Prince of Orange in 1688, and afterwards thrown into the form of an act of Parliament called the Bill of Rights. It is evident, therefore, that, according to their primitive signification, they have no application to constitutions, professedly founded upon the power of the people and executed by their immediate representatives and servants. Here, in strictness, the people surrender nothing; and as they retain everything they have no need of particular reservations. "WE, THE PEOPLE of the United States, to secure the blessings of liberty to ourselves and our posterity, do ordain and establish this Constitution for the United States of America."[3] Here is a better recognition of popular rights than volumes of those aphorisms which make the principal figure in several of our state bills of rights and which would sound much better in a treatise of ethics than in a constitution of government.

But a minute detail of particular rights is certainly far less applicable to a constitution like that under consideration, which is merely intended to regulate the general political interests of the nation, than to a constitution which has the regulation of every species of personal and private concerns. If, therefore, the loud clamors against the plan of the convention, on this score, are well founded, no epithets of reprobation will be too strong for the constitution of this State. But the truth is that both of them contain all which, in relation to their objects, is reasonably to be desired.

I go further and affirm that bills of rights, in the sense and to the extent in which they are contended for, are not only unnecessary in the proposed Constitution but would even be dangerous. They would contain various exceptions to powers not granted; and, on this very account, would afford a colorable pretext to claim more than were granted. For why declare that things shall not be done which there is no power to do? Why, for instance, should it be said that the liberty of the press shall not be restrained, when no power is given by which restrictions may be imposed? I will not contend that such a provision would confer a regulating power; but it is evident that it would furnish, to men disposed to usurp, a plausible pretense for claiming that power. They might urge with a semblance of reason that the Constitution ought not to be charged with the absurdity of providing against the abuse of an authority which was not given, and that the provision against restraining the liberty of the press afforded a clear implication that a power to prescribe proper regulations concerning it was intended to be vested in the national

---

[3] Publius paraphrases the preamble to the Constitution.

government. This may serve as a specimen of the numerous handles which would be given to the doctrine of constructive powers, by the indulgence of an injudicious zeal for bills of rights.

On the subject of the liberty of the press, as much as has been said, I cannot forbear adding a remark or two: in the first place, I observe, that there is not a syllable concerning it in the constitution of this state; in the next, I contend that whatever has been said about it in that of any other state amounts to nothing. What signifies a declaration that "the liberty of the press shall be inviolably preserved"? What is the liberty of the press? Who can give it any definition which would not leave the utmost latitude for evasion? I hold it to be impracticable; and from this I infer that its security, whatever fine declarations may be inserted in any constitution respecting it, must altogether depend on public opinion, and on the general spirit of the people and of the government. And here, after all, as is intimated upon another occasion, must we seek for the only solid basis of all our rights.

There remains but one other view of this matter to conclude the point. The truth is, after all the declamations we have heard, that the Constitution is itself, in every rational sense, and to every useful purpose, a bill of rights. The several bills of rights in Great Britain form its Constitution, and conversely the constitution of each state is its bill of rights. In like manner, the proposed Constitution, if adopted, will be the bill of rights of the Union. Is it one object of a bill of rights to declare and specify the political privileges of the citizens in the structure and administration of the government? This is done in the most ample and precise manner in the plan of the convention; comprehending various precautions for the public security which are not to be found in any of the state constitutions. Is another object of a bill of rights to define certain immunities and modes of proceeding, which are relative to personal and private concerns? This we have seen has also been attended to in a variety of cases in the same plan. Adverting therefore to the substantial meaning of a bill of rights, it is absurd to allege that it is not to be found in the work of the convention. It may be said that it does not go far enough though it will not be easy to make this appear; but it can with no propriety be contended that there is no such thing. It certainly must be immaterial what mode is observed as to the order of declaring the rights of the citizens if they are to be found in any part of the instrument which establishes the government. Whence it must be apparent that much of what has been said on this subject rests merely on verbal and nominal distinctions, entirely foreign from the substance of the thing....

PUBLIUS

Thomas Jefferson to James Madison

July 31, 1788

James Madison wrote to Thomas Jefferson in Paris, where Jefferson was serving as Ambassador, that the U.S. Constitution had been ratified, thus avoiding the danger of a second convention, as well as the adoption of unfriendly amendments as a condition for ratification. Madison was relieved and optimistic. In this response, Jefferson reminded Madison that there was still much work to be done: the Constitution is a "good canvas" that needs to be retouched with a bill of rights. Madison had heard this argument before, but in 1787–1788 he was focused on creating the Constitution, and then seeing it adopted. With the adoption of the Constitution, Madison was finally willing to entertain the idea of adopting a bill of rights. But this adoption, he would argue, must not undermine the Constitution. There was no going back to the Articles of Confederation in the move forward to incorporate a bill of rights. Jefferson, less worried by the dangers of constitutional revision, would soon experience the tumult of the French Revolution.

SOURCE: To James Madison from Thomas Jefferson, 31 July 1788 (*Founders Online*), https://goo.gl/m1Jz4E. For ease of reading, we have added paragraph divisions.

... I sincerely rejoice at the acceptance of our new Constitution by nine states. It is a good canvas, on which some strokes only want retouching. What these are, I think are sufficiently manifested by the general voice from north to south, which calls for a bill of rights. It seems pretty generally understood, that this should go to juries, habeas corpus, standing armies, printing, religion and monopolies. I conceive there may be difficulty in finding general modifications of these, suited to the habits of all the states.

But if such cannot be found, then it is better to establish trials by jury, the right of habeas corpus, freedom of the press and freedom of religion, in all cases, and to abolish standing armies in time of peace, and monopolies in all cases, than not to do it in any. The few cases wherein these things may do evil, cannot be weighed against the multitude wherein the want of them will do evil. In disputes between a foreigner and a native, a trial by jury may be improper. But if this exception cannot be agreed to, the remedy will be to model the jury by giving the *mediatas linguae*,[1] in civil as well as criminal cases. Why suspend the habeas corpus in insurrections and rebellions? The parties who may be arrested, may be charged instantly with a well-defined crime. Of course, the judge will remand them. If the public safety requires that the government should have a man imprisoned on less probable testimony in those than in other emergencies, let him be taken and tried, retaken and retried, while the necessity continues, only giving him redress against the government, for damages. . . .

A declaration, that the federal government will never restrain the presses from printing any thing they please, will not take away the liability of the printers for false facts printed. The declaration that religious faith shall be unpunished, does not give impunity to criminal acts dictated by religious error. The saying there shall be no monopolies, lessens the incitements to ingenuity, which is spurred on by the hope of a monopoly for a limited time, as of 14 years; but the benefit even of limited monopolies is too doubtful to be opposed to that of their general suppression. If no check can be found to keep the number of standing troops within safe bounds, while they are tolerated as far as necessary, abandon them altogether, discipline well the militia, and guard the magazines with them. More than magazine guards will be useless, if few, and dangerous, if many. No European nation can ever send against us such a regular army as we need fear, and it is hard if our militia are not equal to those of Canada or Florida. My idea, then, is that though proper exceptions to these general rules are desirable and probably practicable, yet if the exceptions cannot be agreed on, the establishment of the rules, in all cases, will do ill in very few. I hope, therefore, a bill of rights will be formed to guard the people against the federal government, as they are already guarded against their state governments, in most instances.

The abandoning the principle of necessary rotation in the Senate has, I see, been disapproved by many; in the case of the President, by none. I readily therefore suppose my opinion is wrong, when opposed by the majority as in the former instance, and the totality as in the latter. In this however I should have done it with more complete satisfaction, had we all judged from the same position. . . .

---

[1] Mediatas linguae, a Latin expression meaning "half tongue," indicates that in the criminal trial of a foreigner or alien, a jury has been composed one half of natives and one half of foreigners.

James Madison to Thomas Jefferson

October 17, 1788

J ames Madison responded to Thomas Jefferson's challenges about the absence
of a bill of rights in the newly signed and ratified Constitution (Document 20)
by stating that he had always been in favor of a bill of rights. Scholars have dis-
agreed over Madison's "apparent conversion" in favor a bill of rights. Was Madison flip-flopping from the consistent Wilson-Hamilton line (Documents 10 and
19) that a bill of rights was unnecessary and dangerous because he hoped to win
a seat in the First Congress? Or was he acknowledging the fact that many prominent leaders—including Jefferson—were both in favor of a bill of rights and the
adoption of the Constitution? It is reasonable to read Madison's response, along
with the "little pamphlet herewith enclosed," as a first draft of his more famous
and polished June 8, 1789 speech on behalf of a bill of rights (Document 22).

SOURCE: From James Madison to Thomas Jefferson, 17 October 1788 (*Founders Online*), https://goo.gl/40765p. For ease of reading, we have added paragraph divisions.

... The little pamphlet herewith enclosed will give you a collective view of
the alterations which have been proposed for the new Constitution.[1] Various
and numerous as they appear they certainly omit many of the true grounds of
opposition. The articles relating to treaties, to paper money, and to contracts,
created more enemies than all errors in the system positive and negative put
together. It is true nevertheless that not a few, particularly in Virginia have
contended for the proposed alterations from the most honorable and patriotic motives; and that among the advocates for the Constitution there are
some who wish for further guards to public liberty and individual rights. As
far as these may consist of a constitutional declaration of the most essential
rights, it is probable they will be added; though there are many who think

---

[1] *The Ratifications of the New Federal Constitution, Together with the Amendments,
Proposed by the Several States* (Richmond, 1788)

such addition unnecessary, and not a few who think it misplaced in such a Constitution. There is scarce any point on which the party in opposition is so much divided as to its importance and its propriety.

My own opinion has always been in favor of a bill of rights; provided it be so framed as not to imply powers not meant to be included in the enumeration. At the same time I have never thought the omission a material defect nor been anxious to supply it even by subsequent amendment, for any other reason than that it is anxiously desired by others. I have favored it because I supposed it might be of use, and if properly executed could not be of disservice.

I have not viewed it in an important light.

1. Because I conceive that in a certain degree, though not in the extent argued by Mr. Wilson, the rights in question are reserved by the manner in which the federal powers are granted.

2. Because there is great reason to fear that a positive declaration of some of the most essential rights could not be obtained in the requisite latitude. I am sure that the rights of conscience in particular, if submitted to the public definition would be narrowed much more than they are likely ever to be by an assumed power. One of the objections in New England was that the Constitution by prohibiting religious tests opened a door for Jews, Turks and infidels.

3. Because the limited powers of the federal government and the jealousy of the subordinate governments, afford a security which has not existed in the case of the state governments, and exists in no other.

4. Because experience proves the inefficacy of a bill of rights on those occasions when its control is most needed. Repeated violations of these parchment barriers have been committed by overbearing majorities in every State. In Virginia I have seen the bill of rights violated in every instance where it has been opposed to a popular current. Notwithstanding the explicit provision contained in that instrument for the rights of conscience it is well known that a religious establishment would have taken place and on narrower ground than was then proposed, notwithstanding the additional obstacle which the law has since created. Wherever the real power in a government lies, there is the danger of oppression.

In our governments the real power lies in the majority of the community, and the invasion of private rights is chiefly to be apprehended, not from acts of government contrary to the sense of its constituents, but from acts in which the government is the mere instrument of the majority of the constituents. This is a truth of great importance, but not yet sufficiently attended to: and is probably more strongly impressed on my mind by facts, and reflections suggested by them, than on yours which has contemplated abuses of power issuing from a very different quarter. Wherever there is an interest and power to do wrong, wrong will generally be done, and not less readily by a powerful and interested party than by a powerful and interested prince. The difference, so far as it relates to the superiority of republics over monarchies, lies in the less degree of probability that interest may prompt abuses of power in the former than in the latter; and in the security in the former against oppression of more than the smaller part of the society, whereas in the former [that is, latter] it may be extended in a manner to the whole. The difference so far as it relates to the point in question—the efficacy of a bill of rights in controlling abuses of power—lies in this: that in a monarchy the latent force of the nation is superior to that of the sovereign, and a solemn charter of popular rights must have a great effect, as a standard for trying the validity of public acts, and a signal for rousing and uniting the superior force of the community; whereas in a popular government, the political and physical power may be considered as vested in the same hands, that is in a majority of the people, and consequently the tyrannical will of the sovereign is not to be controlled by the dread of an appeal to any other force within the community.

What use then it may be asked can a bill of rights serve in popular governments? I answer the two following which though less essential than in other governments, sufficiently recommend the precaution.

1. The political truths declared that in solemn manner acquire by degrees the character of fundamental maxims of free government, and as they become incorporated with the national sentiment, counteract the impulses of interest and passion.

2. Although it be generally true as above stated that the danger of oppression lies in the interested majorities of the people rather than in usurped acts of the government, yet there may be occasions on which the evil may spring from the latter sources; and on such, a bill of rights will be a good ground for an appeal to the sense of the community. Perhaps too there may be a certain degree of danger, that a succession of artful and ambitious rulers, may by gradual and well-timed advances, finally erect an independent government on the subversion of liberty. Should this danger exist at all, it is prudent to

guard against it, especially when the precaution can do no injury. At the same time I must own that I see no tendency in our governments to danger on that side. It has been remarked that there is a tendency in all governments to an augmentation of power at the expense of liberty. But the remark as usually understood does not appear to me well founded. Power when it has attained a certain degree of energy and independence goes on generally to further degrees. But when below that degree, the direct tendency is to further degrees of relaxation, until the abuses of liberty beget a sudden transition to an undue degree of power. With this explanation the remark may be true; and in the latter sense only is it in my opinion applicable to the governments in America. It is a melancholy reflection that liberty should be equally exposed to danger whether the government have too much or too little power; and that the line which divides these extremes should be so inaccurately defined by experience.

Supposing a bill of rights to be proper the articles which ought to compose it, admit of much discussion. I am inclined to think that absolute restrictions in cases that are doubtful, or where emergencies may overrule them, ought to be avoided. The restrictions however strongly marked on paper will never be regarded when opposed to the decided sense of the public; and after repeated violations in extraordinary cases, they will lose even their ordinary efficacy. Should a rebellion or insurrection alarm the people as well as the government, and a suspension of the habeas corpus be dictated by the alarm, no written prohibitions on earth would prevent the measure. Should an army in time of peace be gradually established in our neighborhood by Britain or Spain, declarations on paper would have as little effect in preventing a standing force for the public safety. The best security against these evils is to remove the pretext for them.

With regard to monopolies they are justly classed among the greatest nuisances in government. But is it clear that as encouragements to literary works and indigenous discoveries, they are not too valuable to be wholly renounced? Would it not suffice to reserve in all cases a right to the public to abolish the privilege at a price to be specified in the grant of it? Is there not also infinitely less danger of this abuse in our governments than in most others? Monopolies are sacrifices of the many to the few. Where the power is in the few it is natural for them to sacrifice the many to their own partialities and corruptions. Where the power, as with us, is in the many not in the few, the danger cannot be very great that the few will be thus favored. It is much more to be dreaded that the few will be unnecessarily sacrificed to the many.

Representative James Madison
Argues for a Bill of Rights

June 8, 1789

O n June 8, 1789, James Madison finally persuaded the Federalist majority in the House of Representatives to take seriously the issue of amending the Constitution. Some doubted that amendments were needed while others argued that consideration be postponed. Madison insisted that Congress pay attention to the wishes of "a respectable number of our constituents," and that the Representatives "incorporate such amendments in the Constitution as will secure those rights, which they consider as not sufficiently guarded." Of Madison's nine amendment proposals—which were thirty-nine when counted separately—none aimed at altering the structure or powers of the general government. Madison wanted to open up the Constitution and insert these thirty-nine specific changes where appropriate. The longest and most important proposal was the fourth; it actually adds ten additional exceptions to the powers of Congress in Article I, section 9. The list in this article contains seven of the ten amendments adopted subsequently by the state legislatures.

Madison defended these "moderate" and "proper" revisions. Madison, in effect, revisited the exchanges he had with Jefferson (Documents 16, 20, 21); this time Jefferson's arguments blended with Madison's own to form a "conclusive" new defense that is neither wholly Madisonian nor wholly Jeffersonian, but a mixture of both. The blending is clearest in the fifth proposition. Madison mixed Jefferson's notion that "a bill of rights is what the people are entitled to against every government on earth" (Document 16), with his own concern that the greatest danger to liberty is at the state level. The result is a proposition declaring that "no state shall violate the equal right of the conscience, freedom of the press, or trial by jury in criminal cases; because it is proper that every government should be disarmed of powers which trench upon those particular rights." This proposition was defeated in the Senate (Document 24). Madison also attempted to introduce into the Preamble ideas drawn from the Declaration of Independence (Appendix C).

SOURCE: Annals of Congress, ed. Joseph Gales, (Washington, DC: Government Printing Office, 1834), I: 448–459, 467–468; available online from A Century of Lawmaking for a New

Nation: U.S. Congressional Documents and Debates, 1774–1875. Library of Congress, https:// goo.gl/Sgwu9b.

Mr. MADISON—...I will state my reasons why I think it proper to propose amendments; and state the amendments themselves, so far as I think they ought to be proposed. If I thought I could fulfill the duty which I owe to myself and my constituents, to let the subject pass over in silence, I most certainly should not trespass upon the indulgence of this House. But I cannot do this; and am therefore compelled to beg a patient hearing to what I have to lay before you. And I do most sincerely believe, that if Congress will devote but one day to this subject, so far as to satisfy the public that we do not disregard their wishes, it will have a salutary influence on the public councils, and prepare the way for a favorable reception of our future measures. It appears to me that this House is bound by every motive of prudence, not to let the first session pass over without proposing to the state legislatures, some things to be incorporated into the Constitution, that will render it as acceptable to the whole people of the United States, as it has been found acceptable to a majority of them. I wish, among other reasons why something should be done, that those who have been friendly to the adoption of this Constitution, may have the opportunity of proving to those who were opposed to it that they were as sincerely devoted to liberty and a republican government, as those who charged them with wishing the adoption of this Constitution in order to lay the foundation of an aristocracy or despotism. It will be a desirable thing to extinguish from the bosom of every member of the community any apprehensions that there are those among his countrymen who wish to deprive them of the liberty for which they valiantly fought and honorably bled. And if there are amendments desired of such a nature as will not injure the Constitution, and they can be engrafted so as to give satisfaction to the doubting part of our fellow-citizens, the friends of the federal government will evince that spirit of deference and concession for which they have hitherto been distinguished.

It cannot be a secret to the gentlemen in this House, that, notwithstanding the ratification of this system of government by eleven of the thirteen United States, in some cases unanimously, in others by large majorities; yet still there is a great number of our constituents who are dissatisfied with it; among whom are many respectable for their talents and patriotism, and respectable for the jealousy they have for their liberty, which, though mistaken in its object, is laudable in its motive. There is a great body of the people falling under this description, who at present feel much inclined to join their support to the cause of Federalism, if they were satisfied on this one point. We ought not to disregard their inclination, but, on principles of amity and moderation, conform to their wishes, and expressly declare the great rights of mankind secured under this Constitution. The acquiescence which our fellow citizens show under the government, calls upon us for a like return of moderation. But perhaps there is a stronger motive than this for our going into a consideration of the subject. It is to provide those securities for liberty which are required by a part of the community; I allude in a particular manner to those two states[1] who have not thought fit to throw themselves into the bosom of the confederacy. It is a desirable thing, on our part as well as theirs, that a re-union should take place as soon as possible. I have no doubt, if we proceed to take those steps which would be prudent and requisite at this juncture, that in a short time we should see that disposition prevailing in those states that are not come in, that we have seen prevailing in those states which have embraced the Constitution.

But I will candidly acknowledge, that, over and above all these considerations, I do conceive that the Constitution may be amended; that is to say, if all power is subject to abuse, that then it is possible the abuse of the powers of the general government may be guarded against in a more secure manner than is now done, while no one advantage arising from the exercise of that power shall be damaged or endangered by it. We have in this way something to gain, and, if we proceed with caution, nothing to lose. And in this case it is necessary to proceed with caution; for while we feel all these inducements to go into a revisal of the Constitution, we must feel for the Constitution itself, and make that revisal a moderate one. I should be unwilling to see a door opened for a re-consideration of the whole structure of the government—for a re-consideration of the principles and the substance of the powers given; because I doubt, if such a door were opened, we should be very likely to stop at that point which would be safe to the government itself. But I do wish to see a door opened to consider, so far as to incorporate those provisions for the security of rights, against which I believe no serious objection has been made by any class of our constituents: such as would be likely to meet

---

[1] North Carolina, which ratified November 21, 1789, and Rhode Island, which ratified May 29, 1790

with the concurrence of two-thirds of both houses, and the approbation of three-fourths of the state legislatures. I will not propose a single alteration which I do not wish to see take place, as intrinsically proper in itself, or proper because it is wished for by a respectable number of my fellow-citizens; and therefore I shall not propose a single alteration but is likely to meet the concurrence required by the Constitution. There have been objections of various kinds made against the Constitution. Some were leveled against its structure, because the President was without a council; because the Senate, which is a legislative body, had judicial powers in trials on impeachments; and because the powers of that body were compounded in other respects, in a manner that did not correspond with a particular theory; because it grants more power than is supposed to be necessary for every good purpose, and controls the ordinary powers of the state governments. I know some respectable characters who opposed this government on these grounds; but I believe that the great mass of the people who opposed it, disliked it because it did not contain effectual provision against the encroachments on particular rights, and those safeguards which they have been long accustomed to have interposed between them and the magistrate who exercised the sovereign power: nor ought we to consider them safe, while a great number of our fellow-citizens think these securities necessary.

It has been a fortunate thing that the objection to the government has been made on the ground I stated; because it will be practicable, on that ground, to obviate the objection, so far as to satisfy the public mind that their liberties will be perpetual, and this without endangering any part of the Constitution, which is considered as essential to the existence of the government by those who promoted its adoption.

The amendments which have occurred to me, proper to be recommended by Congress to the state legislatures, are these:

First. That there be prefixed to the Constitution a declaration, that all power is originally vested in, and consequently derived from, the people.[2]

That government is instituted and ought to be exercised for the benefit of the people; which consists in the enjoyment of life and liberty, with the right of acquiring and using property, and generally of pursuing and obtaining happiness and safety.

That the people have an indubitable, unalienable, and indefeasible right

---

[2] Compare the language of this and the following two paragraphs to the second paragraph of the Declaration of Independence, Appendix C.

to reform or change their government, whenever it be found adverse or inadequate to the purposes of its institution.

Secondly. That in article 1st, section 2, clause 3, these words be struck out, to wit: "The number of Representatives shall not exceed one for every thirty thousand, but each state shall have at least one Representative, and until such enumeration shall be made;" and in place thereof be inserted these words, to wit: "After the first actual enumeration, there shall be one Representative for every thirty thousand, until the number amounts to—, after which the proportion shall be so regulated by Congress, that the number shall never be less than—, nor more than—, but each state shall, after the first enumeration, have at least two Representatives; and prior thereto."

Thirdly. That in article 1st, section 6, clause 1, there be added to the end of the first sentence, these words, to wit: "But no law varying the compensation last ascertained shall operate before the next ensuing election of Representatives."

Fourthly. That in article 1st, section 9, between clauses 3 and 4, be inserted these clauses, to wit: The civil rights of none shall be abridged on account of religious belief or worship, nor shall any national religion be established, nor shall the full and equal rights of conscience be in any manner, or on any pretext, infringed.

The people shall not be deprived or abridged of their right to speak, to write, or to publish their sentiments; and the freedom of the press, as one of the great bulwarks of liberty, shall be inviolable.

The people shall not be restrained from peaceably assembling and consulting for their common good; nor from applying to the legislature by petitions, or remonstrances for redress of their grievances.

The right of the people to keep and bear arms shall not be infringed; a well armed and well regulated militia being the best security of a free country: but no person religiously scrupulous of bearing arms shall be compelled to render military service in person.

No soldier shall in time of peace be quartered in any house without the consent of the owner; nor at any time, but in a manner warranted by law.

No person shall be subject, except in cases of impeachment, to more than one punishment, or one trial for the same offence; nor shall be compelled to be a witness against himself; nor be deprived of life, liberty, or property, without due process of law; nor be obliged to relinquish his property, where it may be necessary for public use, without a just compensation.

Excessive bail shall not be required, nor excessive fines imposed, nor cruel and unusual punishments inflicted.

The rights of the people to be secured in their persons, their houses, their papers, and their other property, from all unreasonable searches and seizures, shall not be violated by warrants issued without probable cause, supported by oath or affirmation, or not particularly describing the places to be searched, or the persons or things to be seized.

In all criminal prosecutions, the accused shall enjoy the right to a speedy and public trial, to be informed of the cause and nature of the accusation, to be confronted with his accusers, and the witnesses against him; to have a compulsory process for obtaining witnesses in his favor; and to have the assistance of counsel for his defense.

The exceptions here or elsewhere in the Constitution, made in favor of particular rights, shall not be so construed as to diminish the just importance of other rights retained by the people, or as to enlarge the powers delegated by the Constitution; but either as actual limitations of such powers, or as inserted merely for greater caution.

Fifthly. That in article 1st, section 10, between clauses 1 and 2, be inserted this clause, to wit:

No state shall violate the equal rights of conscience, or the freedom of the press, or the trial by jury in criminal cases.

Sixthly. That, in article 3d, section 2, be annexed to the end of clause 2d, these words, to wit:

But no appeal to such court shall be allowed where the value in controversy shall not amount to—dollars: nor shall any fact triable by jury, according to the course of common law, be otherwise re-examinable than may consist with the principles of common law.

Seventhly. That in article 3d, section 2, the third clause be struck out, and in its place be inserted the clauses following, to wit:

The trial of all crimes (except in cases of impeachments, and cases arising in the land or naval forces, or the militia when on actual service, in time of war or public danger) shall be by an impartial jury of freeholders of the vicinage, with the requisite of unanimity for conviction, of the right of challenge, and other accustomed requisites; and in all crimes punishable with loss of life or member, presentment or indictment by a grand jury shall be an essential preliminary, provided that in cases of crimes committed within any county which may be in possession of an enemy, or in which a general insurrection may prevail, the trial may by law be authorized in some other county of the same state, as near as may be to the seat of the offence.

In cases of crimes committed not within any county, the trial may by law be in such county as the laws shall have prescribed. In suits at common law, between man and man, the trial by jury, as one of the best securities to the rights of the people, ought to remain inviolate.

Eighthly. That immediately after article 6th, be inserted, as article 7th, the clauses following, to wit:

The powers delegated by this Constitution are appropriated to the departments to which they are respectively distributed: so that the Legislative department shall never exercise the powers vested in the Executive or Judicial, nor the Executive exercise the powers vested in the Legislative or Judicial, nor the Judicial exercise the powers vested in the Legislative or Executive departments.

The powers not delegated by this Constitution, nor prohibited by it to the states, are reserved to the states respectively.

Ninthly. That article 7th, be numbered as article 8th.

The first of these amendments, relates to what may be called a bill of rights. I will own that I never considered this provision so essential to the federal Constitution as to make it improper to ratify it, until such an amendment was added; at the same time, I always conceived, that in a certain form, and to a certain extent, such a provision was neither improper nor altogether useless. I am aware that a great number of the most respectable friends to the government, and champions for republican liberty, have thought such a provision not only unnecessary, but even improper, nay, I believe some have gone so far as to think it even dangerous.[3] Some policy has been made use of, perhaps, by gentlemen on both sides of the question: I acknowledge the ingenuity of those arguments which were drawn against the Constitution, by a comparison with the policy of Great Britain, in establishing a declaration of rights; but there is too great a difference in the case to warrant the comparison: therefore, the arguments drawn from that source were in a great measure inapplicable. In the declaration of rights which that country has established, the truth is, they have gone no farther than to raise a barrier against the power of the crown; the power of the legislature is left altogether indefinite. Although I know whenever the great rights, the trial by jury, freedom of the press, or liberty of conscience, came in question in that body, the invasion of them is resisted by able advocates, yet their Magna Charta[4] does not contain any one provision for the security of those rights, respecting which the people of America are most alarmed. The freedom of the press and

---

[3] This was once Madison's view. See Document 16.

[4] A charter of rights, or limits on the king's power, agreed to by King John of England and certain barons in 1215

rights of conscience, those choicest privileges of the people, are unguarded in the British Constitution.

But although the case may be widely different, and it may not be thought necessary to provide limits for the legislative power in that country, yet a different opinion prevails in the United States. The people of many states, have thought it necessary to raise barriers against power in all forms and departments of government, and I am inclined to believe, if once bills of rights are established in all the states as well as the federal Constitution, we shall find, that, although some of them are rather unimportant, yet, upon the whole, they will have a salutary tendency. It may be said, in some instances, they do no more than state the perfect equality of mankind. This, to be sure, is an absolute truth, yet it is not absolutely necessary to be inserted at the head of a Constitution.

In some instances they assert those rights which are exercised by the people in forming and establishing a plan of government. In other instances, they specify those rights which are retained when particular powers are given up to be exercised by the legislature. In other instances, they specify positive rights, which may seem to result from the nature of the compact. Trial by jury cannot be considered as a natural right, but a right resulting from a social compact, which regulates the action of the community, but is as essential to secure the liberty of the people as any one of the pre-existent rights of nature. In other instances, they lay down dogmatic maxims with respect to the construction of the government; declaring, that the Legislative, Executive, and Judicial branches, shall be kept separate and distinct. Perhaps the best way of securing this in practice is, to provide such checks as will prevent the encroachment of the one upon the other.

But, whatever may be the form which the several states have adopted in making declarations in favor of particular rights, the great object in view is to limit and qualify the powers of government, by excepting out of the grant of power those cases in which the government ought not to act, or to act only in particular mode. They point these exceptions sometimes against the abuse of the Executive power, sometimes against the Legislative, and, in some cases, against the community itself; or, in other words, against the majority in favor of the minority.

In our government it is, perhaps, less necessary to guard against the abuse in the Executive department than any other; because it is not the stronger branch of the system, but the weaker. It therefore must be leveled against the Legislative, for it is the most powerful, and most likely to be abused, because it is under the least control. Hence, so far as a declaration of rights can tend

to prevent the exercise of undue power, it cannot be doubted but such declaration is proper. But I confess that I do conceive, that in a government modified like this of the United States, the great danger lies rather in the abuse
of the community than in the Legislative body. The prescriptions in favor
of liberty ought to be leveled against that quarter where the greatest danger
lies, namely, that which possesses the highest prerogative of power. But this is
not found in either the Executive or Legislative departments of government,
but in the body of the people, operating by the majority against the minority.

It may be thought all paper barriers against the power of the community
are too weak to be worthy of attention. I am sensible they are not so strong as
to satisfy gentlemen of every description who have seen and examined thor-
oughly the texture of such a defense; yet, as they have a tendency to impress
some degree of respect for them, to establish the public opinion in their favor,
and rouse the attention of the whole community, it may be one means to control the majority from those acts to which they might be otherwise inclined.

It has been said, by way of objection to a bill of rights, by many respectable
gentlemen out of doors, and I find opposition on the same principles likely
to be made by gentlemen on this floor, that they are unnecessary articles
of a republican government, upon the presumption that the people have
those rights in their own hands, and that is the proper place for them to
rest. It would be a sufficient answer to say, that this objection lies against
such provisions under the state government, as well as under the general
government; and there are, I believe, but few gentlemen who are inclined to
push their theory so far as to say that a declaration of rights in those cases
is either ineffectual or improper. It has been said, that in the federal government they are unnecessary, because the powers are enumerated, and it
follows, that all that are not granted by the Constitution are retained; that
the Constitution is a bill of powers, the great residuum being the rights of
the people; and, therefore, a bill of rights cannot be so necessary as if the
residuum was thrown into the hands of the government. I admit that these
arguments are not entirely without foundation; but they are not conclusive
to the extent which has been supposed. It is true, the powers of the general
government are circumscribed, they are directed to particular objects; but
even if government keeps within those limits, it has certain discretionary
powers with respect to the means, which may admit of abuse to a certain
extent, in the same manner as the powers of the state governments under
their constitutions may to an indefinite extent; because in the Constitution
of the United States, there is a clause granting to Congress the power to make
all laws which shall be necessary and proper for carrying into execution all

the powers vested in the government of the United States, or in any department or officer thereof; this enables them to fulfill every purpose for which the government was established. Now, may not laws be considered necessary and proper by Congress, (for it is them who are to judge of the necessity and propriety to accomplish those special purposes which they may have in contemplation,) which laws in themselves are neither necessary or proper; as well as improper laws could be enacted by the state legislatures, for fulfilling the more extended objects of those governments? I will state an instance, which I think in point, and proves that this might be the case. The general government has a right to pass all laws which shall be necessary to collect its revenue; the means for enforcing the collection are within the direction of the legislature: may not general warrants be considered necessary for this purpose, as well as for some purposes which it was supposed at the framing of their constitutions the state governments had in view? If there was reason for restraining the state governments from exercising this power, there is like reason for restraining the federal government.

It may be said, indeed it has been said, that a bill of rights is not necessary, because the establishment of this government has not repealed those declarations of rights which are added to the several state constitutions; that those rights of the people which had been established by the most solemn act, could not be annihilated by a subsequent act of that people, who meant and declared at the head of the instrument, that they ordained and established a new system, for the express purpose of securing to themselves and posterity the liberties they had gained by an arduous conflict.

I admit the force of this observation, but I do not look upon it to be conclusive. In the first place, it is too uncertain ground to leave this provision upon, if a provision is at all necessary to secure rights so important as many of those I have mentioned are conceived to be, by the public in general, as well as those in particular who opposed the adoption of this Constitution. Beside some states have no bills of rights, there are others provided with very defective ones, and there are others whose bills of rights are not only defective, but absolutely improper; instead of securing some in the full extent which republican principles would require, they limit them too much to agree with the common ideas of liberty.

It has been objected also against a bill of rights, that, by enumerating particular exceptions to the grant of power, it would disparage those rights which were not placed in that enumeration; and it might follow by implication, that those rights which were not singled out, were intended to be assigned into the hands of the general government, and were consequently insecure.

This is one of the most plausible arguments I have ever heard urged against the admission of a bill of rights into this system; but, I conceive, that may be guarded against. I have attempted it, as gentlemen may see by turning to the last clause of the fourth resolution.[5]

It has been said that it is unnecessary to load the Constitution with this provision, because it was not found effectual in the constitution of the particular states. It is true, there are a few particular states in which some of the most valuable articles have not, at one time or other, been violated; but it does not follow but they may have, to a certain degree, a salutary effect against the abuse of power. If they are incorporated into the Constitution, independent tribunals of justice will consider themselves in a peculiar manner the guardians of those rights; they will be an impenetrable bulwark against every assumption of power in the Legislative or Executive; they will be naturally led to resist every encroachment upon rights expressly stipulated for in the Constitution by the declaration of rights. Besides this security, there is a great probability that such a declaration in the federal system would be enforced; because the state legislatures will jealously and closely watch the operations of this government, and be able to resist with more effect every assumption of power, than any other power on earth can do; and the greatest opponents to a federal government admit the state legislatures to be sure guardians of the people's liberty. I conclude, from this view of the subject, that it will be proper in itself, and highly politic, for the tranquility of the public mind, and the stability of the government, that we should offer something, in the form I have proposed, to be incorporated in the system of government, as a declaration of the rights of the people.

In the next place, I wish to see that part of the Constitution revised which declares that the number of Representatives shall not exceed one for every thirty thousand persons, and allows one Representative to every state that ranks below that proportion. If we attend to the discussion of this subject, which has taken place in the state conventions, and even in the opinion of the friends to the Constitution, an alteration here is proper. It is the sense of the people of America, that the number of Representatives ought to be increased, but particularly that it should not to be left in the discretion of the government to diminish them, below that proportion which is certainly in the power of the legislature, as the Constitution now stands; and they may, as the population of the country increases, increase the House of Representatives to a very unwieldy degree. I confess I always thought this part

_____

[5] For another version of this argument, see Document 18.

of the Constitution defective, though not dangerous; and that it ought to be particularly attended to whenever Congress should go into the consideration of amendments.

There are several minor cases enumerated in my proposition, in which I wish also to see some alteration take place. That article which leaves it in the power of the legislature to ascertain its own emolument, is one to which I allude. I do not believe this is a power which, in the ordinary course of government, is likely to be abused. Perhaps of all the powers granted, it is the least likely to abuse; but there is a seeming impropriety in leaving any set of men without control to put their hand in the public coffers, to take out money to put in their own pockets; there is a seeming indecorum in such power, which leads me to propose a change. We have a guide to this alteration in several of the amendments which the different conventions have proposed. I have gone, therefore, so far as to fix it, that no law varying the compensation, shall operate until there is a change in the legislature; in which case it cannot be for the particular benefit of those who are concerned in determining the value of the service.

I wish, also, in revising the Constitution, we may throw into that section, which interdicts the abuse of certain powers in the state legislatures, some other provisions of equal if not greater importance than those already made. The words, "No state shall pass any bill of attainder, ex post facto law," &c., were wise and proper restrictions in the Constitution. I think there is more danger of those powers being abused by the state governments than by the government of the United States. The same may be said of other powers which they possess, if not controlled by the general principle, that laws are unconstitutional which infringe the rights of the community. I should, therefore, wish to extend this interdiction, and add, as I have stated in the 5th resolution, that no state shall violate the equal right of conscience, freedom of the press, or trial by jury in criminal cases; because it is proper that every government should be disarmed of powers which trench upon those particular rights. I know, in some of the state constitutions, the power of the government is controlled by such a declaration; but others are not. I cannot see any reason against obtaining even a double security on those points; and nothing can give a more sincere proof of the attachment of those who opposed this Constitution to these great and important rights, than to see them join in obtaining the security I have now proposed; because it must be admitted, on all hands, that the state governments are as liable to attack these invaluable privileges as the general government is, and therefore ought to be as cautiously guarded against.

I think it will be proper, with respect to the judiciary powers, to satisfy the public mind on those points which I have mentioned. Great inconvenience has been apprehended to suitors from the distance they would be dragged to obtain justice in the Supreme Court of the United States, upon an appeal on an action for a small debt. To remedy this, declare that no appeal shall be made unless the matter in controversy amounts to a particular sum; this, with the regulations respecting jury trials in criminal cases, and suits at common law, it is to be hoped, will quiet and reconcile the minds of the people to that part of the Constitution.

I find, from looking into the amendments proposed by the state conventions, that several are particularly anxious that it should be declared in the Constitution, that the powers not therein delegated, should be reserved to the several states. Perhaps words which may define this more precisely than the whole of the instrument now does, may be considered as superfluous. I admit they may be deemed unnecessary; but there can be no harm in making such a declaration, if gentlemen will allow that the fact is as stated. I am sure I understand it so, and do therefore propose it.

These are the points on which I wish to see a revision of the Constitution take place. How far they will accord with the sense of this body, I cannot take upon me absolutely to determine; but I believe every gentleman will readily admit that nothing is in contemplation, so far as I have mentioned, that can endanger the beauty of the government in any one important feature, even in the eyes of its most sanguine admirers. I have proposed nothing that does not appear to me as proper in itself, or eligible as patronized by a respectable number of our fellow-citizens; and if we can make the Constitution better in the opinion of those who are opposed to it, without weakening its frame, or abridging its usefulness in the judgment of those who are attached to it, we act the part of wise and liberal men to make such alterations as shall produce that effect.

Having done what I conceived was my duty, in bringing before this House the subject of amendments, and also stated such as I wish for and approve, and offered the reasons which occurred to me in their support, I shall content myself, for the present, with moving "that a committee be appointed to consider of and report such amendments as ought to be proposed by Congress to the legislatures of the states, to become, if ratified by three-fourths thereof, part of the Constitution of the United States." By agreeing to this motion, the subject may be going on in the committee, while other important business is proceeding to a conclusion in the House. I should advocate greater dispatch in the business of amendments, if I was not convinced of the absolute necessity there is of pursuing the organization of the government;[6] because I think we should obtain the confidence of our fellow-citizens, in proportion as we fortify the rights of the people against the encroachments of the Government.

[Debate ensued over the merits of sending Madison's proposals to a select committee.]

Mr. MADISON found himself unfortunate in not satisfying gentlemen with respect to the mode of introducing the business; he thought, from the dignity and the peculiarity of the subject, that it ought to be referred to a committee of the whole. He accordingly made that motion first, but finding himself not likely to succeed in that way, he had changed his ground. Fearing again to be discomfited, he would change his mode, and move the propositions he had stated before, and the House might do what they thought proper with them. He accordingly moved the propositions by way of resolutions to be adopted by the House....

Mr. LAWRENCE[7] moved to refer Mr. Madison's motion to the committee of the whole on the state of the Union....

At length Mr. Lawrence's motion was agreed to, and Mr. Madison's propositions were ordered to be referred to a committee of the whole. Adjourned.

---

[6] Between the date of Madison's speech on the Bill of Rights and the end of September 1789, Congress established the State Department, War Department, Treasury, and the federal judiciary, as well as passing other legislation to establish and fund government operations.

[7] John Lawrence or Laurence (1750–1810), a Revolutionary war veteran, was a New York lawyer and politician who served in the Continental Congress, House of Representatives, and Senate.

The House Version

July 28, August 13–24, 1789

T he members of the House of Representatives of the First Congress sent
James Madison's proposals (Document 22) to a select committee. The House
debated the report of the committee between August 13 and 24, 1789. The report
and these debates show that Madison, although initially successful in shaping the
content of the Bill of Rights, was ultimately unsuccessful in his attempt to "interweave" the proposed alterations into the body of the original Constitution. Also,
thanks to his old nemesis from the Constitutional Convention of 1787, Roger Sherman, he failed to alter the Preamble of the Constitution to incorporate, expressly,
the principles of the Declaration of Independence (Appendix C). In short, he was
unsuccessful in creating a new founding that incorporated in one document the
Declaration, the original Constitution, and the Bill of Rights.

He was successful, however, in limiting the scope of the alterations in the Constitution to a friendly declaration of rights rather than unfriendly amendments of
the structure and powers of the federal government (Documents 17, 18). He also
persuaded the House to include what he considered to be his three most important items in a declaration of rights—conscience, press, and jury—as restrictions
on both the federal and the state governments. Note the subtle changes in language concerning the two religion clauses as Madison's proposals made their way
through the debates in the House.

SOURCE: *Congress of the United States In the House of Representatives, Tuesday, the 27th of July:*
Mr. Vining, from the Committee of eleven, to whom it was referred to take the subject of
amendments to the constitution of the United States, genera. (New York: Thomas Greenleaf,
1789) Library of Congress, goo.gl/roAqoH; *Annals of Congress*, ed. Joseph Gales, (Washington, DC: Government Printing Office, 1834), vol. I: 734–735, 742–743, 744, 746–747,
808); available online from *A Century of Lawmaking for a New Nation: U.S. Congressional
Documents and Debates, 1774–1875.* Library of Congress, goo.gl/VV4HTS. See also *The Essential Bill of Rights*, ed. Gordon Lloyd and Margie Lloyd (Lanham, MD: University Press of
America, 1998), 345–353.

Report of the House Select Committee, July 28, 1789

MR. VINING, from the committee of eleven, to whom it was referred to take the subject of AMENDMENTS to the CONSTITUTION of the UNITED STATES, generally into their consideration, and to report thereupon, made a report, which was read, and is as followeth:

In the introductory paragraph before the words, "We the people," add, "government being intended for the benefit of the people, and the rightful establishment thereof being derived from their authority alone."

ART. I, SEC. 2, PAR. 3—Strike out all between the words, "direct" and "and until such," and instead thereof insert, "After the first enumeration there shall be one Representative for every thirty thousand until the number shall amount to one hundred; after which the proportion shall be so regulated by Congress that the number of Representatives shall never be less than one hundred, nor more than one hundred and seventy-five, but each State shall always have at least one Representative."

ART. I, SEC. 6—Between the words, "United States," and "shall in all cases," strike out "they," and insert, "But no law varying the compensation shall take effect until an election of Representatives shall have intervened. The members."

ART. I, SEC. 9—Between PAR. 2 and 3 insert "No religion shall be established by law, nor shall the equal rights of conscience be infringed."

"The freedom of speech, and of the press, and the right of the people peaceably to assemble and consult for their common good, and to apply to the government for redress of grievances, shall not be infringed."

"A well-regulated militia, composed of the body of the people, being the best security of a free state, the right of the people to keep and bear arms shall not be infringed, but no person religiously scrupulous shall be compelled to bear arms."

"No soldier shall in time of peace be quartered in any house without the consent of the owner, nor in time of war but in a manner to be prescribed by law."

"No person shall be subject, except in case of impeachment, to more than one trial or one punishment for the same offence, nor shall be compelled to be a witness against himself, nor be deprived of life, liberty, or property without due process of law; nor shall private property be taken for public use without just compensation."

"Excessive bail shall not be required, nor excessive fines imposed, nor cruel and unusual punishment inflicted."

"The right of the people to be secure in their person, houses, papers and effects, shall not be violated by warrants issuing, without probable cause supported by oath or affirmation, and not particularly describing the places to be searched, and the persons or things to be seized."

"The enumeration in this Constitution of certain rights shall not be construed to deny or disparage others retained by the people."

ART. 1, SEC. 10, between the 1st and 2d PAR. insert, "No state shall infringe the equal rights of conscience, nor the freedom of speech, or of the press, nor of the right of trial by jury in criminal cases."

ART. 3, SEC. 2, add to the 2d PAR. "But no appeal to such court shall be allowed, where the value in controversy shall not amount to one thousand dollars; nor shall any fact, triable by a jury according to the course of the common law, be otherwise re-examinable than according to the rules of common law."

ART. 3, SEC. 2—Strike out the whole of the 3d paragraph, and insert: "In all criminal prosecutions the accused shall enjoy the right to a speedy and public trial, to be informed of the nature and cause of the accusation, to be confronted with the witnesses against him, to have compulsory process for obtaining witnesses in his favor, and to have the assistance of counsel for his defense."

"The trial of all crimes (except in cases of impeachment, and in cases arising in the land or naval forces, or in the militia, when in actual service in time of war or public danger) shall be by an impartial jury of freeholders of the vicinage, with the requisite of unanimity for conviction, the right of challenge and other accustomed requisites; and no person shall be held to answer for a capital, or otherwise infamous crime, unless on a presentment or indictment by a grand jury; but if a crime be committed in a place in the possession of an enemy, or in which an insurrection may prevail, the indictment and trial may by law be authorized in some other place within the same state; and if it be committed in a place not within a state, the indictment and trial may be at such place or places as the law may have directed."

"In suits at common law the right of trial by jury shall be preserved."

"Immediately after ART. 6, the following to be inserted as ART. 7:

"The powers delegated by this Constitution to the government of the United States, shall be exercised as therein appropriated, so that the Legislative shall never exercise the powers vested in the Executive or the Judicial; nor the Executive the powers vested in the Legislative or Judicial; nor the Judicial the powers vested in the Legislative or Executive."

"The powers not delegated by this Constitution, nor prohibited by it to the states, are reserved to the States respectively."

ART. 7 to be made ART. 8.

House Debates Select Committee Report, August 13–24, 1789

Thursday, August 13

The House then resolved itself into a committee of the whole, Mr. BOUDI-NOT in the chair, and took the amendments under consideration.

The first article ran thus: "In the introductory paragraph of the Constitution, before the words 'We the people,' add 'government being intended for the benefit of the people, and the rightful establishment thereof being derived from their authority alone.'

MR. SHERMAN. I believe, Mr. Chairman, this is not the proper mode of amending the Constitution. We ought not to interweave our propositions into the work itself, because it will be destructive of the whole fabric. We might as well endeavor to mix brass, iron, and clay, as to incorporate such heterogeneous articles, the one contradictory to the other. Its absurdity will be discovered by comparing it with a law. Would any legislature endeavor to introduce into a former act a subsequent amendment, and let them stand so connected? When an alteration is made in an act, it is done by way of supplement; the latter act always repealing the former in every specified case of difference.

Besides this, sir, it is questionable whether we have the right to propose amendments in this way. The Constitution is the act of the people, and ought to remain entire. But the amendments will be the act of the state governments. Again, all the authority we possess is derived from that instrument; if we mean to destroy the whole, and establish a new Constitution, we remove the basis on which we mean to build. For these reasons, I will move to strike out that paragraph and substitute another.

The paragraph proposed was to the following effect:

Resolved, by the Senate and House of Representatives of the United States in Congress assembled, That the following articles be proposed as amendments to the Constitution, and when ratified by three-fourths of the state legislatures shall become valid to all intents and purposes, as part of the same.

Under this title, the amendments might come in nearly as stated in the report, only varying the phraseology so as to accommodate them to a supplementary form.

Mr. MADISON. Form, sir, is always of less importance than the substance; but on this occasion I admit that form is of some consequence, and it will be well for the House to pursue that which, upon reflection, shall appear to be the most eligible. Now it appears to me, that there is a neatness and propriety in incorporating the amendments into the Constitution itself; in that case, the system will remain uniform and entire; it will certainly be more simple when the amendments are interwoven into those parts to which they naturally belong, than it will if they consist of separate and distinct parts. We shall then be able to determine its meaning without references or comparison; whereas, if they are supplementary, its meaning can only be ascertained by a comparison of the two instruments, which will be a very considerable embarrassment. It will be difficult to ascertain to what parts of the instrument the amendments particularly refer; they will create unfavorable comparisons; whereas, if they are placed upon the footing here proposed, they will stand upon as good foundation as the original work. Nor is it so uncommon a thing as gentlemen suppose; systematic men frequently take up the whole law, and, with its amendments and alterations, reduce it into one act. I am not, however, very solicitous about the form, provided the business is but well completed....

Mr. SHERMAN. If I had looked upon this question as a mere matter of form, I should not have brought it forward, or troubled the committee with such a lengthy discussion. But, sir, I contend that amendments made in the way proposed by the committee are void. No gentleman ever knew an addition and alteration introduced into an existing law, and that any part of such law was left in force; but if it was improved or altered by a supplemental act, the original retained all its validity and importance, in every case where the two were not incompatible. But if these observations alone should be thought insufficient to support my motion, I would desire gentlemen to consider the authorities upon which the two Constitutions are to stand. The original was established by the people at large, by conventions chosen by them for the express purpose. The preamble to the Constitution declares the act; but will it be a truth in ratifying the next Constitution, which is to be done perhaps by the State Legislatures, and not conventions chosen for the purpose? Will gentlemen say it is "We the people" in this case? Certainly they cannot; for, by the present Constitution, we, nor all the legislatures in the Union together, do not possess the power of repealing it. All that is granted us by the 5th article is, that whenever we shall think it necessary, we may propose amendments to the Constitution; not that we may propose to repeal the old, and substitute a new one.

Gentlemen say, it would be convenient to have it in one instrument, that people might see the whole at once; for my part, I view no difficulty on this point. The amendments reported are a declaration of rights; the people are secure in them, whether we declare them or not; the last amendment but one provides that the three branches of government shall each exercise its own rights. This is well secured already; and, in short, I do not see that they lessen the force of any article in the Constitution; if so, there can be little more difficulty in comprehending them whether they are combined in one, or stand distinct instruments....

Mr. SHERMAN. The gentlemen who oppose the motion say we contend for matter of form; they think it nothing more. Now we say we contend for substance, and therefore cannot agree to amendments in this way. If they are so desirous of having the business completed, they had better sacrifice what they consider but a matter of indifference to gentlemen, to go more unanimously along with them in altering the Constitution.

The question on Mr. SHERMAN'S motion was now put and lost....

Friday, August 14

...Mr. MADISON. If it be a truth, and so self-evident that it cannot be denied; if it be recognized, as is the fact in many of the state constitutions; and if it be desired by three important states to be added to this; I think they must collectively offer a strong inducement to the mind desirous of promoting harmony to acquiesce with the report; at least some strong arguments should be brought forward to show the reason why it is improper.

My worthy colleague says the original expression is neat and simple; that loading it with more words may destroy the beauty of the sentence; and others say it is unnecessary, as the paragraph is complete without it. Be it so in their opinion; yet still it appears important in the estimation of three States that this solemn truth should be inserted in the Constitution. For my part, sir, I do not think the association of ideas anywise unnatural; it reads very well in this place; so much so, that I think gentlemen, who admit it should come in somewhere else, will be puzzled to find a better place.

Mr. SHERMAN thought they ought not to come in this place. The people of the United States have given their reasons for doing a certain act. Here we propose to come in and give them a right to do what they did on motives which appeared to them sufficient to warrant their determination; to let them know that they had a right to exercise a natural and inherent privilege, which they have asserted in a solemn ordination and establishment of the Constitution.

Now, if this right is indefeasible, and the people have recognized it in practice, the truth is better asserted than it can be by any words whatever. The words "We the people," in the original Constitution, are as copious and expressive as possible; any addition will only drag out the sentence without illuminating it; for these reasons it may be hoped the committee will reject the proposed amendment.

The question on the first paragraph of the report was put and carried in the affirmative, twenty-seven to twenty-three....

Wednesday, August 19

... Mr. SHERMAN renewed his motion for adding the amendments to the Constitution by way of supplement.

Hereupon, ensued a debate similar to what took place in the Committee of the Whole, [see Thursday, August 13, above] but, on the question, Mr. SHERMAN'S motion was carried by two-thirds of the House; in consequence it was agreed to.

The first proposition of amendment [see Friday, August 14, above] was rejected, because two-thirds of the members present did not support it....

[Editor's Note. The House, as the last order of business on Saturday, August 22, directed Representatives Benson, Sherman, and Sedgwick "to arrange" the agreed upon amendments "and make a report thereof."]

Monday, August 24

Mr. BENSON, from the committee appointed for the purpose, reported an arrangement of the articles of amendment to the Constitution of the United States, as agreed to by the House on Friday last....

House Approves Seventeen Amendments, August 24, 1789

Article the First

After the first enumeration, required by the first Article of the Constitution, there shall be one Representative for every thirty thousand, until the number shall amount to one hundred, after which the proportion shall be so regulated by Congress, that there shall be not less than one hundred Representatives, nor less than one Representative for every forty thousand persons, until the number of Representatives shall amount to two hundred, after which the proportion shall be so regulated by Congress, that there shall not be less than two hundred Representatives, nor less than one Representative for every fifty thousand persons.

Article the Second

No law varying the compensation to the members of Congress, shall take effect, until an election of Representatives shall have intervened.

Article the Third

Congress shall make no law establishing religion or prohibiting the free exercise thereof, nor shall the rights of conscience be infringed.

Article the Fourth

The freedom of speech, and of the press, and the right of the people peaceably to assemble, and consult for their common good, and to apply to the government for a redress of grievances, shall not be infringed.

Article the Fifth

A well-regulated militia, composed of the body of the people, being the best security of a free state, the right of the people to keep and bear arms, shall not be infringed, but no one religiously scrupulous of bearing arms, shall be compelled to render military service in person.

Article the Sixth

No soldier shall, in time of peace, be quartered in any house without the consent of the owner, nor in time of war, but in a manner to be prescribed by law.

Article the Seventh

The right of the people to be secure in their persons, houses, papers and effects, against unreasonable searches and seizures, shall not be violated, and no warrants shall issue, but upon probable cause supported by oath or affirmation, and particularly describing the place to be searched, and the persons or things to be seized.

Article the Eighth

No person shall be subject, except in case of impeachment, to more than one trial, or one punishment for the same offence, nor shall be compelled in any criminal case, to be a witness against himself, nor be deprived of life, liberty or property, without due process of law; nor shall private property be taken for public use without just compensation.

Article the Ninth

In all criminal prosecutions, the accused shall enjoy the right to a speedy and public trial, to be informed of the nature and cause of the accusation, to be confronted with the witnesses against him, to have compulsory process for obtaining witnesses in his favor, and to have the assistance of counsel for his defense.

Article the Tenth

The trial of all crimes (except in cases of impeachment, and in cases arising in the land or naval forces, or in the militia when in actual service in time of war or public danger) shall be by an impartial jury of the vicinage, with the requisite of unanimity for conviction, the right of challenge, and other accustomed requisites; and no person shall be held to answer for a capital, or otherways infamous crime, unless on a presentment or indictment by a grand jury; but if a crime be committed in a place in the possession of an enemy, or in which an insurrection may prevail, the indictment and trial may by law be authorized in some other place within the same state.

Article the Eleventh

No appeal to the Supreme Court of the United States, shall be allowed, where the value in controversy shall not amount to one thousand dollars, nor shall any fact, triable by a jury according to the course of the common law, be otherwise re-examinable, than according to the rules of common law.

Article the Twelfth

In suits at common law, the right of trial by jury shall be preserved.

Article the Thirteenth

Excessive bail shall not be required, nor excessive fines imposed, nor cruel and unusual punishments inflicted.

Article the Fourteenth

No state shall infringe the right of trial by jury in criminal cases, nor the rights of conscience, nor the freedom of speech, or of the press.

Article the Fifteenth

The enumeration in the Constitution of certain rights, shall not be construed to deny or disparage others retained by the people.

Article the Sixteenth

The powers delegated by the Constitution to the government of the United States, shall be exercised as therein appropriated, so that the Legislative shall never exercise the powers vested in the Executive or Judicial; nor the Executive the powers vested in the Legislative or Judicial; nor the Judicial the powers vested in the Legislative or Executive.

Article the Seventeenth

The powers not delegated by the Constitution, nor prohibited by it, to the states, are reserved to the states respectively.

The Senate Version

August 25–September 9, 1789

U nfortunately, there is no official record of the debates in the Senate. There are, however, brief summary remarks in the Senate Journal and from interested parties. Notice the care taken over the language in the religion clauses. Most importantly, in reducing and combining the seventeen House amendments into twelve amendments, the Senate eliminated limitations on the power of state governments over freedom of conscience, freedom of the press, and jury trials that James Madison and the House had approved. In addition, the Senate combined into one article the formerly separately proposed restraints on the federal government with respect to religion, press, and association. Not unexpectedly, there was niggling over the wording of the religion clauses.

Among the most important Senate alterations to the House proposals was the deletion of what Madison considered to be the cornerstone of his thirty-nine Bill of Rights proposals—restraints on the state governments—for Madison had come to agree with Thomas Jefferson that every government should have a bill of rights, including the state governments. Madison expressed his disapproval of the Senate version to Edmund Pendleton on September 14, 1789: "The Senate have sent back the plan of amendments with some alterations which strike in my opinion at the most salutary articles." Still, he went along with the Senate alterations.

SOURCE: *Senate Journal, First Congress, First Session,* A Century of Lawmaking for a New Nation: U.S. Congressional Documents and Debates, 1774–1875, Library of Congress, https://goo.gl/DKsP5C.

Senate Journal of the Debates over the Bill of Rights in the First Congress

September 3, 1789

The Senate resumed the consideration of the resolve of the House of Representatives on the Amendments to the Constitution of the United States.

On motion, to adopt the second article proposed in the resolve of the House of Representatives, amended as follows—

To strike out these words, "To the Members of Congress," and insert "for the service of the Senate and House of Representatives of the United States,"

It passed in the affirmative.

On motion, to amend article the third, and to strike out these words, "religion or prohibiting the free exercise thereof," and insert, "one religious sect or society in preference to others,"

It passed in the negative.[1]

On motion, for reconsideration,

It passed in the affirmative.

On motion, that article the third be stricken out,

It passed in the negative.

On motion, to adopt the following, in lieu of the third article, "Congress shall not make any law, infringing the rights of conscience, or establishing any religious sect or society,"

It passed in the negative.

On motion, to amend the third article, to read thus—"Congress shall make no law establishing any particular denomination of religion in preference to another, or prohibiting the free exercise thereof, nor shall the rights of conscience be infringed"—

On the question upon the third article as it came from the House of Representatives—

It passed in the negative.

On motion, to adopt the third article proposed in the resolve of the House of Representatives, amended by striking out these words—"Nor shall the rights of conscience be infringed"—

It passed in the affirmative.

September 7, 1789

On motion, to add the following to the proposed amendments, to wit:

"That the third section of the sixth article of the Constitution of the United States, ought to be amended by inserting the word OTHER between the words "no" and "religious"—

It passed in the negative.

---

[1] That is, it did not pass.

September 9, 1789

Proceeded in the consideration of the resolve of the House of Representatives of the 24th of August, "On article to be proposed to the legislatures of the several states as amendments to the Constitution of the United States"—

On motion, to amend article the third, to read as follows:

"Congress shall make no law establishing articles of faith or a mode of worship, or prohibiting the free exercise of religion, or abridging the freedom of speech, or the press, or the right of the people peaceably to assemble and petition to the government for the redress of grievances"—

It passed in the affirmative.

Senate Approves Twelve Amendments

September 9, 1789

Article the First

After the first enumeration, required by the first article of the Constitution, there shall be one Representative for every thirty thousand, until the number shall amount to one hundred; to which number one Representative shall be added for every subsequent increase of forty thousand, until the Representatives shall amount to two hundred, to which number one Representative shall be added for every subsequent increase of sixty thousand persons.

Article the Second

No law, varying the compensation for the services of the Senators and Representatives, shall take effect, until an election of Representatives shall have intervened.

Article the Third

Congress shall make no law establishing articles of faith, or a mode of worship, or prohibiting the free exercise of religion, or abridging the freedom of speech, or of the press, or the right of the people peaceably to assemble, and to petition to the government for a redress of grievances.

Article the Fourth

A well-regulated militia, being necessary to the security of a free State, the right of the people to keep and bear arms, shall not be infringed.

Article the Fifth

No soldier shall, in time of peace, be quartered in any house, without the consent of the owner, nor in time of war, but in a manner to be prescribed by law.

Article the Sixth

The right of the people to be secure in their persons, houses, papers, and effects, against unreasonable searches and seizures, shall not be violated, and no warrants shall issue, but upon probable cause, supported by oath or affirmation, and particularly describing the place to be searched, and the persons or things to be seized.

Article the Seventh

No person shall be held to answer for a capital, or otherwise infamous crime, unless on a presentment or indictment of a grand jury, except in cases arising in the land or naval forces, or in the militia, when in actual service in time of war or public danger; nor shall any person be subject for the same offence to be twice put in jeopardy of life or limb; nor shall be compelled in any criminal case, to be a witness against himself, nor be deprived of life, liberty or property, without due process of law; nor shall private property be taken for public use without just compensation.

Article the Eighth

In all criminal prosecutions, the accused shall enjoy the right to a speedy and public trial, to be informed of the nature and cause of the accusation, to be confronted with the witnesses against him, to have compulsory process for obtaining witnesses in his favor, and to have the assistance of counsel for his defense.

Article the Ninth

In suits at common law, where the value in controversy shall exceed twenty dollars, the right of trial by jury shall be preserved, and no fact, tried by a jury, shall be otherwise re-examined in any court of the United States, than according to the rules of the common law.

Article the Tenth

Excessive bail shall not be required, nor excessive fines imposed, nor cruel and unusual punishments inflicted.

Article the Eleventh

The enumeration in the Constitution of certain rights, shall not be construed to deny or disparage others retained by the people.

Article the Twelfth

The powers not delegated to the United States by the Constitution, nor prohibited by it to the states, are reserved to the states respectively, or to the people.

The Congress Sends Twelve Amendments to the States

September 25, 1789

The House and Senate Conference Committee agreed on September 25, 1789 to reconcile the differences between the House and Senate versions. The House members agreed with the Senate changes with one exception: there was a last successful attempt to change the language of the religion clauses. The House appointed James Madison (Virginia), Roger Sherman (Connecticut), and John Vining (Delaware) to the Conference Committee. The Senate appointed Oliver Ellsworth (Connecticut), Charles Carroll (Maryland), and William Paterson (New Jersey). So four of the six members of the Conference Committee were framers in Philadelphia. The House agreed to the reduction of the number of amendments by the Senate from seventeen to twelve in exchange for a concession on the language of the religion clauses. We think it highly unlikely that these four framers would recommend alterations that would conflict with the original Constitution. We also find it fascinating that Madison and Sherman were quarreling over the merits of a large republic and small republic on June 6, 1787 at the Constitutional Convention, and here they are putting the final touches to the religious clauses two and a half years later.

John Beckley, Clerk of the House, introduced the "Articles to be proposed to the legislatures of the several states, as amendments to the Constitution of the United States." He informed the Senate, that the House of Representatives had receded from its disagreement to the amendments insisted on by the Senate: "Provided that the two articles which by the amendments of the Senate are now proposed to be inserted as the third and eighth articles," should be amended and combined into one, to read as follows: "Congress shall make no law respecting an establishment of religion, or prohibiting the free exercise thereof; or abridging the freedom of speech, or of the press; or the right of the people peaceably to assemble, and petition the government for a redress of grievances."

SOURCE: The Essential Bill of Rights, ed. Gordon Lloyd and Margie Lloyd, (Lanham, MD: University Press of America, 1998), 353–355.

Article the first ... After the first enumeration required by the first article of the Constitution, there shall be one Representative for every thirty thousand, until the number shall amount to one hundred, after which, the proportion shall be so regulated by Congress, that there shall be not less than one hundred Representatives, nor less than one Representative for every forty thousand persons, until the number of Representatives shall amount to two hundred, after which the proportion shall be so regulated by Congress, that there shall not be less than two hundred Representatives, nor more than one Representative for every fifty thousand persons.

Article the second ... No law, varying the compensation for the services of the Senator and Representatives, shall take effect, until an election of Representatives shall have intervened.

Article the third ... Congress shall make no law respecting an establishment of religion, or prohibiting the free exercise thereof; or abridging the freedom of speech, or of the press; or the right of the people peaceably to assemble, and to petition the government for a redress of grievances.

Article the fourth ... A well-regulated militia, being necessary to the security of a free state, the right of the people to keep and bear arms, shall not be infringed.

Article the fifth ... No soldier shall, in time of peace be quartered in any house, without the consent of the owner, nor in time of war, but in a manner to be prescribed by law.

Article the sixth ... The right of the people to be secure in their persons, houses, papers, and effects, against unreasonable searches and seizures, shall not be violated, and no warrants shall issue, but upon probable cause, supported by oath or affirmation, and particularly describing the place to be searched, and the persons or things to be seized.

Article the seventh ... No person shall be held to answer for a capital, or otherwise infamous crime, unless on a presentment or indictment of a grand jury, except in cases arising in the land or naval forces, or in the militia, when in actual service in time of war or public danger; nor shall any person be subject for the same offence to be twice put in jeopardy of life or limb, nor shall be compelled in any criminal case to be a witness against himself, nor be deprived of life, liberty, or property, without due process of law; nor shall private property be taken for public use without just compensation.

Article the eighth ... In all criminal prosecutions, the accused shall enjoy the right to a speedy and public trial, by an impartial jury of the state and district wherein the crime shall have been committed, which district shall have been previously ascertained by law, and to be informed of the nature and cause of the accusation; to be confronted with the witnesses against him; to have compulsory process for obtaining witnesses in his favor, and to have the assistance of counsel for his defense.

Article the ninth ... In suits at common law, where the value in controversy shall exceed twenty dollars, the right of trial by jury shall be preserved, and no fact tried by a jury, shall be otherwise re-examined in any court of the United States, than according to the rules of the common law.

Article the tenth ... excessive bail shall not be required, nor excessive fines imposed, nor cruel and unusual punishments inflicted.

Article the eleventh ... The enumeration in the Constitution, of certain rights, shall not be construed to deny or disparage others retained by the people.

Article the twelfth ... The powers not delegated to the United States by the Constitution, nor prohibited by it to the states, are reserved to the states respectively, or to the people.

DOCUMENT 26

Amendments I–X: The Bill of Rights

December 15, 1791

The American story of the origin and politics of the Bill of Rights involves a conceptual shift of immense consequences: what began in the 13th century as a protection of the few against the one, had become in America by 1791 the protection of the few against a tyrannical legislative majority! And with this conceptual shift, there was also a potential institutional shift away from the legislative branch as the enforcer of rights of the people to the courts as the primary guardians of individual rights. This was one of Thomas Jefferson's main contributions to the conversation with James Madison, who asked Jefferson who would enforce these paper rights against the majority (Document 21). Jefferson also concurred with Madison that the Legislative and not the Executive branch was the most dangerous branch (Documents 16 and 20). Madison came to recognize that a bill of rights could be more than a "mere parchment" barrier when elected officials overstepped their boundaries (Document 22).

There are no extant documents that record the discussions over the adoption of the Bill of Rights. Secretary of State Jefferson's Tabulation of the State Votes on Amendments to the Constitution, 1789–91, reads thus: New Jersey (November 20, 1789); Maryland (December 19, 1789); North Carolina (December 22, 1789); South Carolina (January 19, 1790); New Hampshire (January 25, 1790); Delaware (January 28, 1790); Pennsylvania (March 10, 1790); New York (March 27, 1790); Rhode Island (June 11, 1790); Vermont (November 3, 1791); Virginia (December 15, 1791).

Massachusetts, Georgia, and Connecticut did not ratify the first ten amendments at the time they were proposed (but did ratify them in 1939 in commemoration of the 150th anniversary of the adoption of the Bill of Rights by the First Congress). Since three states abstained, all the other eleven states needed to vote yes on every clause for all twelve to pass. Vermont was added as the fourteenth state on March 4, 1791, thus changing the number of states needed to ratify from nine to eleven. If only one of the eleven states objected to one of the twelve amendments then that particular amendment would not passed.

Unanimity over all twelve Amendments did not occur. The first and second amendments went down to defeat. We can conclude that eleven states voted "yes" *on all of the other amendments. Thus, the Third Amendment became the First Amendment.*

Writing to George Washington on December 5, 1789, Madison explained the "great difficulty" in securing early ratification in Virginia: "The difficulty started against the amendments is really unlucky, and the more to be regretted as it springs from a friend to the Constitution." Representative John Dawson confirms why Virginia did not ratify earlier in a letter to Madison on December 17, 1789: "The amendments recommended by Congress were taken up and all of them passed our House. ... The Senate amended the resolution by postponing the consideration of the 3d, 11th, & 12th, until the next session of assembly.... We adhered, and so did they. A conference took place, and both houses remained obstinate, consequently the whole resolution was lost, and none of the amendments will be adopted by this assembly."

SOURCE: *The Bill of Rights: a Transcription*, America's Founding Documents, National Archives, https://www.archives.gov/founding-docs/bill-of-rights-transcript. The capitalization and punctuation in this version is from the enrolled original of the Joint Resolution of Congress proposing the Bill of Rights, which is on permanent display in the Rotunda of the National Archives Building, Washington, D.C.

Amendment I

Congress shall make no law respecting an establishment of religion, or prohibiting the free exercise thereof; or abridging the freedom of speech, or of the press; or the right of the people peaceably to assemble, and to petition the Government for a redress of grievances.

Amendment II

A well regulated Militia, being necessary to the security of a free State, the right of the people to keep and bear Arms, shall not be infringed.

Amendment III

No Soldier shall, in time of peace be quartered in any house, without the consent of the Owner, nor in time of war, but in a manner to be prescribed by law.

Amendment IV

The right of the people to be secure in their persons, houses, papers, and effects, against unreasonable searches and seizures, shall not be violated, and no Warrants shall issue, but upon probable cause, supported by Oath or affirmation, and particularly describing the place to be searched, and the persons or things to be seized.

Amendment V

No person shall be held to answer for a capital, or otherwise infamous crime, unless on a presentment or indictment of a Grand Jury, except in cases arising in the land or naval forces, or in the Militia, when in actual service in time of War or public danger; nor shall any person be subject for the same offence to be twice put in jeopardy of life or limb; nor shall be compelled in any criminal case to be a witness against himself, nor be deprived of life, liberty, or property, without due process of law; nor shall private property be taken for public use, without just compensation.

Amendment VI

In all criminal prosecutions, the accused shall enjoy the right to a speedy and public trial, by an impartial jury of the State and district wherein the crime shall have been committed, which district shall have been previously ascertained by law, and to be informed of the nature and cause of the accusation; to be confronted with the witnesses against him; to have compulsory process for obtaining witnesses in his favor, and to have the Assistance of Counsel for his defence.

Amendment VII

In Suits at common law, where the value in controversy shall exceed twenty dollars, the right of trial by jury shall be preserved, and no fact tried by a jury, shall be otherwise re-examined in any Court of the United States, than according to the rules of the common law.

Amendment VIII

Excessive bail shall not be required, nor excessive fines imposed, nor cruel and unusual punishments inflicted.

Amendment IX

The enumeration in the Constitution, of certain rights, shall not be construed to deny or disparage others retained by the people.

Amendment X

The powers not delegated to the United States by the Constitution, nor prohibited by it to the States, are reserved to the States respectively, or to the people.

Thematic Index

The Colonial Heritage

A New and More Noble Course: Creating Republican Governments

The Bill of Rights and Ratification of the Constitution

The Bill of Rights and the First Congress

Study Questions

For each of the documents in this collection, we suggest below in section A questions relevant for that document alone and in section B questions that require comparison between documents.

1. The Massachusetts Body of Liberties, December 1641

A. What rights are protected in this colonial document? How are they protected?

B. What differences and similarities exist in the Massachusetts Body of Liberties and the early state constitutions as far as the type of rights are concerned? For example, does the Massachusetts Body of Liberties refer to freedom of conscience and freedom of the press? See Documents 3, 5, and 6.

2. The Maryland Act Concerning Religion, April 21, 1649

A. Does it strike you as odd that the Maryland Act can simultaneously proclaim the establishment of the Christian religion and the toleration of religion as central principles?

B. Compare the Maryland Act with the early state constitutions and Madison's Memorial and Remonstrance. See Documents 3, 4, 5, 6, and 7.

3. Virginia Declaration of Rights and Constitution, June 12 and 29, 1776

A. Does it seem curious that a) the Virginia Declaration and the Virginia Constitution were written two weeks apart and that b) both preceded the passage of the Declaration of Independence? According to these two documents, what is the purpose of government? What is the role of the legislature, executive, and judiciary in the newly adopted Virginia Constitution? What sort of "republicanism" do these two documents express? Is it surprising that the Declaration of Rights precedes the Constitution?

B. By what authority was the Virginia Declaration of Rights and Constitution initiated and adopted? Compare and contrast the content of the Virginia Declaration of Rights with colonial and other state based documents. See Documents 1, 2, 4, and 6.

4. The New Jersey Constitution, July 3, 1776

A. New Jersey was the first state to incorporate a declaration of rights within the body of the constitution itself. Does it matter where the declaration is located in the constitution? What does the New Jersey Constitution have to say about religious rights?

B. What difference, if any, does it make if the declaration of rights is at the beginning or inserted into the document? Compare with Documents 3, 5, and 6. Is it odd that both the Virginia and New Jersey declarations were written before the Declaration of Independence?

5. The Pennsylvania Declaration of Rights and Constitution, September 28, 1776

A. To what extent does the Pennsylvania document embrace both the common law tradition and the new natural rights tradition?

B. John Adams judged that the Pennsylvania Bill of Rights "is taken almost verbatim from that of Virginia." Is Adams correct? See Document 3.

6. The Massachusetts Declaration of Rights and Constitution, March 2, 1780

A. How is it possible that the people have a right to require of the citizens to support, financially, the establishment of public religion? No one particular sect was given preference over another; all were "equally under the protection of the law" and, thus, the "free exercise" of religion was protected. Explain this explicit association between free exercise of religion and equality under the law.

B. Following Virginia and Pennsylvania, the need for "piety, justice, moderation, temperance, industry, and frugality" was listed in the Bill of Rights. Are these six virtues compatible with the two religion clauses? See Documents 3, 5, and 7.

7. James Madison's Memorial And Remonstrance, June 20, 1785

A. How does Madison remind the legislators of 1783 that they were undermining the very principles of freedom of conscience that Virginians adopted in 1776?

B. Is Madison's *Memorial and Remonstrance* out of touch with the religion clauses of the state constitutions? See Documents 3–6.

8. The Northwest Ordinance, July 13, 1787

A. What sort of country do the framers of the Northwest Ordinance envision for the next generation of Americans?

B. How do the statements on behalf of individual religious rights and the public support of religion compare with the statements found in Documents 3–6?

9. Objections at the Constitutional Convention, September 10, 12, 15, and 17, 1787

A. Are there similarities among the objections to the Constitution listed by Edmund Randolph, Elbridge Gerry, and George Mason? Does their dissent demonstrate an admirable feature of the American experiment? Other delegates had reservations, yet they still signed.

B. Does it strike you as odd that Edmund Randolph, who introduced and defended the Virginia Plan, objected to signing the Constitution? How do these dissents on behalf of a bill of rights compare and contrast with earlier the documents in this collection? See Documents 3–7.

10. James Wilson's State House Speech, October 6, 1787

A. This speech by Wilson upset a lot of prominent opposition politicians and writers. What is so provocative about this speech?

B. What is the central argument of the Antifederalist opposition? See Documents 11–14.

11. *The Federal Farmer* IV, October 12, 1787

A. The Federal Farmer emphasizes the importance of a bill of rights right at the start of the ratifying campaign. What are his arguments in favor of a bill of rights?

B. What are the objections of the Federal Farmer to James Wilson's State House speech? See Document 10. See also Document 19.

12. Richard Henry Lee to Edmund Randolph, October 16, 1787

A. What rights are essential to Richard Henry Lee? Why does the proposed Constitution contain the potentiality to make these rights vulnerable?

B. How do Lee's essential rights compare with those revealed in the Thomas Jefferson–James Madison exchanges? See Documents 16, 20, 21, 22.

13. *An Old Whig* IV, October 27, 1787

A. What are An Old Whig's arguments on behalf of a small republic and a bill of rights?

B. Compare the Old Whig's argument with the argument of *Federalist* 10. See Document 19 in the American Founding Document. Is there a coherence to the Antifederalist argument? See Documents 9, 11, 12, 14, 15.

14. *Brutus* II, November 1, 1787

A. Brutus makes the absence of the Bill of Rights a key issue in the ratification campaign. Does his argument make sense? What rights does Brutus deem "essential"?

B. Are there good reasons why James Wilson and *The Federalist* dismiss the absence of a bill of rights as a vital issue in the proposed Constitution? See Documents 10–12, 19.

15. The Dissent of the Minority of the Convention of Pennsylvania, December 18, 1787

A. What rights did the Pennsylvania Minority consider to be essential?

B. Compare the objections to the Constitution expressed by the Pennsylvania Minority to those raised at the Virginia and New York Ratifying Conventions. See Documents 17 and 18.

16. Thomas Jefferson to James Madison, December 20, 1787

A. What are the six essential rights that Thomas Jefferson states should be included in a Declaration of Rights?

B. Why does Thomas Jefferson disagree with the approach taken by James Wilson in his State House Speech? Which of the six rights mentioned by Jefferson does James Madison endorse? See Documents 10, 21 and 22.

17. The Virginia Ratifying Convention, June 24–June 27, 1788

A. What is the difference between an adoption of the Constitution with previous amendments and adoption with subsequent amendments? Do previous amendments open the door to the possibility of secession? How does the discussion over how to adopt the Constitution enhance our understanding of what is and is not a republican and a federal government?

B. How do the amendment and bill of rights proposals compare and contrast with those listed in the New York ratifying document? See Document 18. Is James Madison's argument against a bill of rights the same as that articulated by James Wilson? See Document 10.

18. New York Ratifying Convention, June 17–July 25, 1788

A. What is the difference between the adoption of the Constitution with previous or conditional amendments and adoption with subsequent or recommended amendments? What are the differences between the content of the twenty-five items in the Bill of Rights proposed at the New York convention and the thirty-one items in the proposed amendments?

B. How do the amendment and bill of rights proposals compare and contrast with those listed in the Virginia ratifying document? See Document 17. How many of the amendment proposals and the Bill of Rights proposals make their way into the Bill of Rights adopted in 1791? See Document 26.

19. *Federalist* 84, July 16, 1788

A. What are the rights that Publius claims are listed in the proposed Constitution? Why does Publius think the Constitution is a bill of rights?

B. To what extent does Publius repeat, or enlarge upon, the arguments made by James Wilson in his State House Speech? See Document 10.

20. Thomas Jefferson to James Madison, July 31, 1788

A. What rights does Thomas Jefferson think that the general voice of America is calling for?

B. Which of these rights does James Madison include in his proposals to Congress? See Document 22. How does Thomas Jefferson's list of rights compare with those requested at the Virginia and New York Ratifying Conventions? See Documents 17 and 18. Has his list expanded or contracted from those contained in Document 16?

21. James Madison to Thomas Jefferson, October 17, 1788

A. Why did James Madison not view the absence of a bill of rights from the proposed Constitution "in an important light"? How did Madison answer his own question: "What use then it may be asked can a bill of rights serve in popular governments"?

B. Compare James Madison's less than enthusiastic support for a bill of rights with James Wilson's State House Speech and Alexander Hamilton's argument in *Federalist* 84. See Documents 10 and 19.

22. Representative James Madison Argues for a Bill of Rights, June 8, 1789

A. What is James Madison's case for the adoption of a bill of rights? Where would he place these thirty-nine constraints on the reach of the federal government? Before the Constitution? Within the Constitution? Or after the Constitution?

B. Compare James Madison's case here for a bill of rights with his exchange with Thomas Jefferson, Did Madison flip-flop? Are there any surprises in his list of thirty-nine rights? Compare with Documents 16, 20, and 21.

23. The House Version, July 28, August 13–24, 1789

A. Why did the House reject James Madison's proposal to incorporate the Bill of Rights into the main body of the original Constitution? What alterations did the House make to Madison's version?

B. How is the House version similar to and different from Madison's June 8 proposals? See Document 22.

24. The Senate Version, August 25–September 9, 1789

A. Why do we know so little about the debates that took place in the Senate? What important contribution, if any, did the Senate make?

B. How is the Senate version similar to and different from the House version and James Madison's June 8 version? See Documents 22 and 23.

25. The Congress sends Twelve Amendments to the States, September 25, 1789

A. Are the changes in the religion clauses significant in the final Congress version?

B. What changes took place in the religion clauses over the course of the First Congress? See Documents 22–24.

26. Amendments I–X: The Bill of Rights, December 15, 1789

A. To what extent is the Bill of Rights an individual rights, a group or associational rights, or a states rights document? Why are there ten rather than twelve or seventeen amendments?

B. Why does the Bill of Rights appear as amendments at the end of the Constitution rather than in the Preamble or in Article I, Section 9 of the Constitution? See Documents 3, 4, 15, 17, 18, 22 and 23.

Declaration of Independence

In CONGRESS, July 4, 1776

The unanimous Declaration of the thirteen united States of America, When in the Course of human events, it becomes necessary for one people to dissolve the political bands which have connected them with another, and to assume among the powers of the earth, the separate and equal station to which the Laws of Nature and of Nature's God entitle them, a decent respect to the opinions of mankind requires that they should declare the causes which impel them to the separation.

We hold these truths to be self-evident, that all men are created equal, that they are endowed by their Creator with certain unalienable Rights, that among these are Life, Liberty and the pursuit of Happiness.—That to secure these rights, Governments are instituted among Men, deriving their just powers from the consent of the governed,—that whenever any Form of Government becomes destructive of these ends, it is the Right of the People to alter or to abolish it, and to institute new Government, laying its foundation on such principles and organizing its powers in such form, as to them shall seem most likely to effect their Safety and Happiness. Prudence, indeed, will dictate that Governments long established should not be changed for light and transient causes; and accordingly all experience hath shewn, that mankind are more disposed to suffer, while evils are sufferable, than to right themselves by abolishing the forms to which they are accustomed. But when a long train of abuses and usurpations, pursuing invariably the same Object evinces a design to reduce them under absolute Despotism, it is their right, it is their duty, to throw off such Government, and to provide new Guards for their future security.—Such has been the patient sufferance of these Colonies; and such is now the necessity which constrains them to alter their former Systems of Government. The history of the present King of Great Britain is a history of repeated injuries and usurpations, all having in direct object the establishment of an absolute Tyranny over these States. To prove this, let Facts be submitted to a candid world.

He has refused his Assent to Laws, the most wholesome and necessary for the public good.

He has forbidden his Governors to pass Laws of immediate and pressing importance, unless suspended in their operation till his Assent should be obtained; and when so suspended, he has utterly neglected to attend to them.

He has refused to pass other Laws for the accommodation of large districts of people, unless those people would relinquish the right of Representation in the Legislature, a right inestimable to them and formidable to tyrants only.

He has called together legislative bodies at places unusual, uncomfortable, and distant from the depository of their public Records, for the sole purpose of fatiguing them into compliance with his measures.

He has dissolved Representative Houses repeatedly, for opposing with manly firmness his invasions on the rights of the people.

He has refused for a long time, after such dissolutions, to cause others to be elected; whereby the Legislative powers, incapable of Annihilation, have returned to the People at large for their exercise; the State remaining in the mean time exposed to all the dangers of invasion from without, and convulsions within.

He has endeavoured to prevent the population of these States; for that purpose obstructing the Laws for Naturalization of Foreigners; refusing to pass others to encourage their migrations hither, and raising the conditions of new Appropriations of Lands.

He has obstructed the Administration of Justice, by refusing his Assent to Laws for establishing Judiciary powers.

He has made Judges dependent on his Will alone, for the tenure of their offices, and the amount and payment of their salaries.

He has erected a multitude of New Offices, and sent hither swarms of Officers to harrass our people, and eat out their substance.

He has kept among us, in times of peace, Standing Armies without the Consent of our legislatures.

He has affected to render the Military independent of and superior to the Civil power.

He has combined with others to subject us to a jurisdiction foreign to our constitution, and unacknowledged by our laws; giving his Assent to their Acts of pretended Legislation:

For Quartering large bodies of armed troops among us:

For protecting them, by a mock Trial, from punishment for any Murders which they should commit on the Inhabitants of these States:

For cutting off our Trade with all parts of the world:

For imposing Taxes on us without our Consent:

For depriving us in many cases, of the benefits of Trial by Jury:

For transporting us beyond Seas to be tried for pretended offences:

For abolishing the free System of English Laws in a neighbouring Province, establishing therein an Arbitrary government, and enlarging its Boundaries so as to render it at once an example and fit instrument for introducing the same absolute rule into these Colonies:

For taking away our Charters, abolishing our most valuable Laws, and altering fundamentally the Forms of our Governments:

For suspending our own Legislatures, and declaring themselves invested with power to legislate for us in all cases whatsoever.

He has abdicated Government here, by declaring us out of his Protection and waging War against us.

He has plundered our seas, ravaged our Coasts, burnt our towns, and destroyed the lives of our people.

He is at this time transporting large Armies of foreign Mercenaries to compleat the works of death, desolation and tyranny, already begun with circumstances of Cruelty & perfidy scarcely paralleled in the most barbarous ages, and totally unworthy the Head of a civilized nation.

He has constrained our fellow Citizens taken Captive on the high Seas to bear Arms against their Country, to become the executioners of their friends and Brethren, or to fall themselves by their Hands.

He has excited domestic insurrections amongst us, and has endeavoured to bring on the inhabitants of our frontiers, the merciless Indian Savages, whose known rule of warfare, is an undistinguished destruction of all ages, sexes and conditions.

In every stage of these Oppressions We have Petitioned for Redress in the most humble terms: Our repeated Petitions have been answered only by repeated injury. A Prince whose character is thus marked by every act which may define a Tyrant, is unfit to be the ruler of a free people.

Nor have We been wanting in attentions to our British brethren. We have warned them from time to time of attempts by their legislature to extend an unwarrantable jurisdiction over us. We have reminded them of the circumstances of our emigration and settlement here. We have appealed to their native justice and magnanimity, and we have conjured them by the ties of our common kindred to disavow these usurpations, which, would inevitably interrupt our connections and correspondence. They too have been deaf to the voice of justice and of consanguinity. We must, therefore, acquiesce in the necessity, which denounces our Separation, and hold them, as we hold the rest of mankind, Enemies in War, in Peace Friends.

We, THEREFORE, the Representatives of the UNITED STATES OF AMERICA, in General Congress, Assembled, appealing to the Supreme Judge of the world for the rectitude of our intentions, do, in the Name, and by Authority of the good People of these Colonies, solemnly publish and declare, That these United Colonies are, and of Right ought to be FREE AND INDEPENDENT STATES; that they are Absolved from all Allegiance to the British Crown, and that all political connection between them and the State of Great Britain, is and ought to be totally dissolved; and that as Free and Independent States, they have full Power to levy War, conclude Peace, contract Alliances, establish Commerce, and to do all other Acts and Things which Independent States may of right do. And for the support of this Declaration, with a firm reliance on the protection of divine Providence, we mutually pledge to each other our Lives, our Fortunes and our sacred Honor.

[Georgia:]
Button Gwinnett
Lyman Hall
George Walton

[North Carolina:]
William Hooper
Joseph Hewes
John Penn

[South Carolina:]
Edward Rutledge
Thomas Heyward, Jr.
Thomas Lynch, Jr.
Arthur Middleton

[Maryland:]
Samuel Chase
William Paca
Thomas Stone
Charles Carroll of Carrollton

[Virginia:]
George Wythe
Richard Henry Lee
Thomas Jefferson

Benjamin Harrison
Thomas Nelson, Jr.
Francis Lightfoot Lee
Carter Braxton

[Pennsylvania:]
Robert Morris
Benjamin Rush
Benjamin Franklin
John Morton
George Clymer
James Smith
George Taylor
James Wilson
George Ross

[Delaware:]
Caesar Rodney
George Read
Thomas McKean

[New York:]
William Floyd
Philip Livingston
Francis Lewis
Lewis Morris

[New Jersey:]
Richard Stockton
John Witherspoon
Francis Hopkinson
John Hart
Abraham Clark

[New Hampshire:]
Josiah Bartlett
William Whipple
Matthew Thornton

[Massachusetts:]
John Hancock
Samuel Adams

John Adams
Robert Treat Paine
Elbridge Gerry

[Rhode Island:]
Stephen Hopkins
William Ellery

[Connecticut:]
Roger Sherman
Samuel Huntington
William Williams
Oliver Wolcott

Constitution of the United States of America

September 17, 1787

[Editors' note: Bracketed sections in the text of the Constitution have been superceded or modified by Constitutional amendments.]

We the People of the United States, in Order to form a more perfect Union, establish Justice, insure domestic Tranquility, provide for the common defence, promote the general Welfare, and secure the Blessings of Liberty to ourselves and our Posterity, do ordain and establish this Constitution for the United States of America.

Article I

Section 1. All legislative Powers herein granted shall be vested in a Congress of the United States, which shall consist of a Senate and House of Representatives.

Section 2. The House of Representatives shall be composed of Members chosen every second Year by the People of the several States, and the Electors in each State shall have the Qualifications requisite for Electors of the most numerous Branch of the State Legislature.

No Person shall be a Representative who shall not have attained to the Age of twenty five Years, and been seven Years a Citizen of the United States, and who shall not, when elected, be an Inhabitant of that State in which he shall be chosen.

[Representatives and direct Taxes shall be apportioned among the several States which may be included within this Union, according to their respective Numbers, which shall be determined by adding to the whole Number of free Persons, including those bound to Service for a Term of Years, and excluding Indians not taxed, three fifths of all other Persons.][1] The actual Enumeration shall be made within three Years after the first

---

[1] modified by Section 2 of the Fourteenth Amendment

Meeting of the Congress of the United States, and within every subsequent Term of ten Years, in such Manner as they shall by Law direct. The Number of Representatives shall not exceed one for every thirty Thousand, but each State shall have at Least one Representative; and until such enumeration shall be made, the State of New Hampshire shall be entitled to chuse three, Massachusetts eight, Rhode-Island and Providence Plantations one, Connecticut five, New-York six, New Jersey four, Pennsylvania eight, Delaware one, Maryland six, Virginia ten, North Carolina five, South Carolina five, and Georgia three.

When vacancies happen in the Representation from any State, the Executive Authority thereof shall issue Writs of Election to fill such Vacancies.

The House of Representatives shall chuse their Speaker and other Officers; and shall have the sole Power of Impeachment.

Section 3. The Senate of the United States shall be composed of two Senators from each State, [*chosen by the Legislature thereof,*][2] for six Years; and each Senator shall have one Vote.

Immediately after they shall be assembled in Consequence of the first Election, they shall be divided as equally as may be into three Classes. The Seats of the Senators of the first Class shall be vacated at the Expiration of the second Year, of the second Class at the Expiration of the fourth Year, and of the third Class at the Expiration of the sixth Year, so that one third may be chosen every second Year; [*and if Vacancies happen by Resignation, or otherwise, during the Recess of the Legislature of any State, the Executive thereof may make temporary Appointments until the next Meeting of the Legislature, which shall then fill such Vacancies.*][3]

No Person shall be a Senator who shall not have attained to the Age of thirty Years, and been nine Years a Citizen of the United States, and who shall not, when elected, be an Inhabitant of that State for which he shall be chosen.

The Vice President of the United States shall be President of the Senate, but shall have no Vote, unless they be equally divided.

The Senate shall chuse their other Officers, and also a President pro tempore, in the Absence of the Vice President, or when he shall exercise the Office of President of the United States.

The Senate shall have the sole Power to try all Impeachments. When sitting for that Purpose, they shall be on Oath or Affirmation. When the

---

[2] superseded by the Seventeenth Amendment
[3] modified by the Seventeenth Amendment

President of the United States is tried, the Chief Justice shall preside: And no Person shall be convicted without the Concurrence of two thirds of the Members present.

Judgment in Cases of Impeachment shall not extend further than to removal from Office, and disqualification to hold and enjoy any Office of honor, Trust or Profit under the United States: but the Party convicted shall nevertheless be liable and subject to Indictment, Trial, Judgment and Punishment, according to Law.

Section 4. The Times, Places and Manner of holding Elections for Senators and Representatives, shall be prescribed in each State by the Legislature thereof; but the Congress may at any time by Law make or alter such Regulations, except as to the Places of chusing Senators.

The Congress shall assemble at least once in every Year, and such Meeting shall be [on the first Monday in December,][4] unless they shall by Law appoint a different Day.

Section 5. Each House shall be the Judge of the Elections, Returns and Qualifications of its own Members, and a Majority of each shall constitute a Quorum to do Business; but a smaller Number may adjourn from day to day, and may be authorized to compel the Attendance of absent Members, in such Manner, and under such Penalties as each House may provide.

Each House may determine the Rules of its Proceedings, punish its Members for disorderly Behaviour, and, with the Concurrence of two thirds, expel a Member.

Each House shall keep a Journal of its Proceedings, and from time to time publish the same, excepting such Parts as may in their Judgment require Secrecy; and the Yeas and Nays of the Members of either House on any question shall, at the Desire of one fifth of those Present, be entered on the Journal.

Neither House, during the Session of Congress, shall, without the Consent of the other, adjourn for more than three days, nor to any other Place than that in which the two Houses shall be sitting.

Section 6. The Senators and Representatives shall receive a Compensation for their Services, to be ascertained by Law, and paid out of the Treasury of the United States. They shall in all Cases, except Treason, Felony and

---

[4] modified by Section 2 of the Twentieth Amendment

Breach of the Peace, be privileged from Arrest during their Attendance at the Session of their respective Houses, and in going to and returning from the same; and for any Speech or Debate in either House, they shall not be questioned in any other Place.

No Senator or Representative shall, during the Time for which he was elected, be appointed to any civil Office under the Authority of the United States, which shall have been created, or the Emoluments whereof shall have been encreased during such time; and no Person holding any Office under the United States, shall be a Member of either House during his Continuance in Office.

Section 7. All Bills for raising Revenue shall originate in the House of Representatives; but the Senate may propose or concur with Amendments as on other Bills.

Every Bill which shall have passed the House of Representatives and the Senate, shall, before it become a Law, be presented to the President of the United States; If he approve he shall sign it, but if not he shall return it, with his Objections to that House in which it shall have originated, who shall enter the Objections at large on their Journal, and proceed to reconsider it. If after such Reconsideration two thirds of that House shall agree to pass the Bill, it shall be sent, together with the Objections, to the other House, by which it shall likewise be reconsidered, and if approved by two thirds of that House, it shall become a Law. But in all such Cases the Votes of both Houses shall be determined by yeas and Nays, and the Names of the Persons voting for and against the Bill shall be entered on the Journal of each House respectively. If any Bill shall not be returned by the President within ten Days (Sundays excepted) after it shall have been presented to him, the Same shall be a Law, in like Manner as if he had signed it, unless the Congress by their Adjournment prevent its Return, in which Case it shall not be a Law.

Every Order, Resolution, or Vote to which the Concurrence of the Senate and House of Representatives may be necessary (except on a question of Adjournment) shall be presented to the President of the United States; and before the Same shall take Effect, shall be approved by him, or being disapproved by him, shall be repassed by two thirds of the Senate and House of Representatives, according to the Rules and Limitations prescribed in the Case of a Bill.

Section 8. The Congress shall have Power To lay and collect Taxes, Duties, Imposts and Excises, to pay the Debts and provide for the common Defence and general Welfare of the United States; but all Duties, Imposts and Excises shall be uniform throughout the United States;

To borrow Money on the credit of the United States;

To regulate Commerce with foreign Nations, and among the several States, and with the Indian Tribes;

To establish an uniform Rule of Naturalization, and uniform Laws on the subject of Bankruptcies throughout the United States;

To coin Money, regulate the Value thereof, and of foreign Coin, and fix the Standard of Weights and Measures;

To provide for the Punishment of counterfeiting the Securities and current Coin of the United States;

To establish Post Offices and post Roads;

To promote the Progress of Science and useful Arts, by securing for limited Times to Authors and Inventors the exclusive Right to their respective Writings and Discoveries;

To constitute Tribunals inferior to the supreme Court;

To define and punish Piracies and Felonies committed on the high Seas, and Offenses against the Law of Nations;

To declare War, grant Letters of Marque and Reprisal, and make Rules concerning Captures on Land and Water;

To raise and support Armies, but no Appropriation of Money to that Use shall be for a longer Term than two Years;

To provide and maintain a Navy;

To make Rules for the Government and Regulation of the land and naval Forces;

To provide for calling forth the Militia to execute the Laws of the Union, suppress Insurrections and repel Invasions;

To provide for organizing, arming, and disciplining, the Militia, and for governing such Part of them as may be employed in the Service of the United States, reserving to the States respectively, the Appointment of the Officers, and the Authority of training the Militia according to the discipline prescribed by Congress;

To exercise exclusive Legislation in all Cases whatsoever, over such District (not exceeding ten Miles square) as may, by Cession of particular States, and the Acceptance of Congress, become the Seat of the Government of the United States, and to exercise like Authority over all Places purchased by the Consent of the Legislature of the State in which the Same shall be, for the Erection of Forts, Magazines, Arsenals, dock-Yards, and other needful Buildings;—And

To make all Laws which shall be necessary and proper for carrying into Execution the foregoing Powers, and all other Powers vested by this Constitution in the Government of the United States, or in any Department or Officer thereof.

Section 9. The Migration or Importation of such Persons as any of the States now existing shall think proper to admit, shall not be prohibited by the Congress prior to the Year one thousand eight hundred and eight, but a Tax or duty may be imposed on such Importation, not exceeding ten dollars for each Person.

The Privilege of the Writ of Habeas Corpus shall not be suspended, unless when in Cases of Rebellion or Invasion the public Safety may require it.

No Bill of Attainder or ex post facto Law shall be passed.

No Capitation, or other direct, Tax shall be laid, unless in Proportion to the Census or Enumeration herein before directed to be taken.[5]

No Tax or Duty shall be laid on Articles exported from any State.

No Preference shall be given by any Regulation of Commerce or Revenue to the Ports of one State over those of another: nor shall Vessels bound to, or from, one State, be obliged to enter, clear, or pay Duties in another.

No Money shall be drawn from the Treasury, but in Consequence of Appropriations made by Law; and a regular Statement and Account of the Receipts and Expenditures of all public Money shall be published from time to time.

No Title of Nobility shall be granted by the United States: And no Person holding any Office of Profit or Trust under them, shall, without the Consent of the Congress, accept of any present, Emolument, Office, or Title, of any kind whatever, from any King, Prince, or foreign State.

Section 10. No State shall enter into any Treaty, Alliance, or Confederation; grant Letters of Marque and Reprisal; coin Money; emit Bills of Credit; make any Thing but gold and silver Coin a Tender in Payment of Debts; pass any Bill of Attainder, ex post facto Law, or Law impairing the Obligation of Contracts, or grant any Title of Nobility.

No State shall, without the Consent of the Congress, lay any Imposts or Duties on Imports or Exports, except what may be absolutely necessary for executing it's inspection Laws: and the net Produce of all Duties and Imposts,

---

[5] modified by the Sixteenth Amendment

laid by any State on Imports or Exports, shall be for the Use of the Treasury of the United States; and all such Laws shall be subject to the Revision and Controul of the Congress.

No State shall, without the Consent of Congress, lay any Duty of Tonnage, keep Troops, or Ships of War in time of Peace, enter into any Agreement or Compact with another State, or with a foreign Power, or engage in War, unless actually invaded, or in such imminent Danger as will not admit of delay.

Article II

Section 1. The executive Power shall be vested in a President of the United States of America. He shall hold his Office during the Term of four Years, and, together with the Vice President, chosen for the same Term, be elected, as follows:

Each State shall appoint, in such Manner as the Legislature thereof may direct, a Number of Electors, equal to the whole Number of Senators and Representatives to which the State may be entitled in the Congress: but no Senator or Representative, or Person holding an Office of Trust or Profit under the United States, shall be appointed an Elector.

[The Electors shall meet in their respective States, and vote by Ballot for two Persons, of whom one at least shall not be an Inhabitant of the same State with themselves. And they shall make a List of all the Persons voted for, and of the Number of Votes for each; which List they shall sign and certify, and transmit sealed to the Seat of the Government of the United States, directed to the President of the Senate. The President of the Senate shall, in the Presence of the Senate and House of Representatives, open all the Certificates, and the Votes shall then be counted. The Person having the greatest Number of Votes shall be the President, if such Number be a Majority of the whole Number of Electors appointed; and if there be more than one who have such Majority, and have an equal Number of Votes, then the House of Representatives shall immediately chuse by Ballot one of them for President; and if no Person have a Majority, then from the five highest on the List the said House shall in like Manner chuse the President. But in chusing the President, the Votes shall be taken by States, the Representation from each State having one Vote; A quorum for this purpose shall consist of a Member or Members from two thirds of the States, and a Majority of all the States shall be necessary to a Choice. In every Case, after the Choice of the President, the Person having the greatest Number of Votes of the Electors shall be the Vice President. But if there should remain two or more who have equal Votes, the Senate shall chuse from them by Ballot the Vice President.]⁶

The Congress may determine the Time of chusing the Electors, and the Day on which they shall give their Votes; which Day shall be the same throughout the United States.

No Persons except a natural born Citizen, or a Citizen of the United States, at the time of the Adoption of this Constitution, shall be eligible to the Office of President; neither shall any Person be eligible to that Office who shall not have attained to the Age of thirty five Years, and been fourteen Years a Resident within the United States.

[In Case of the Removal of the President from Office, or of his Death, Resignation, or Inability to discharge the Powers and Duties of the said Office, the Same shall devolve on the Vice President, and the Congress may by Law provide for the Case of Removal, Death, Resignation or Inability, both of the President and Vice President, declaring what Officer shall then act as President, and such Officer shall act accordingly, until the Disability be removed, or a President shall be elected.]⁷

The President shall, at stated Times, receive for his Services, a Compensation, which shall neither be increased nor diminished during the Period for which he shall have been elected, and he shall not receive within that Period any other Emolument from the United States, or any of them.

Before he enter on the Execution of his Office, he shall take the following Oath or Affirmation:—"I do solemnly swear (or affirm) that I will faithfully execute the Office of President of the United States, and will to the best of my Ability, preserve, protect and defend the Constitution of the United States."

Section 2. The President shall be Commander in Chief of the Army and Navy of the United States, and of the Militia of the several States, when called into the actual Service of the United States; he may require the Opinion, in writing, of the principal Officer in each of the executive Departments, upon any Subject relating to the Duties of their respective Offices, and he shall have Power to grant Reprieves and Pardons for Offences against the United States, except in Cases of Impeachment.

He shall have Power, by and with the Advice and Consent of the Senate,

---

⁶ modifed by the Twelfth Amendment
⁷ modified by the Twenty-Fifth Amendment

to make Treaties, provided two thirds of the Senators present concur; and he shall nominate, and by and with the Advice and Consent of the Senate, shall appoint Ambassadors, other public Ministers and Consuls, Judges of the supreme Court, and all other Officers of the United States, whose Appointments are not herein otherwise provided for, and which shall be established by Law: but the Congress may by Law vest the Appointment of such inferior Officers, as they think proper, in the President alone, in the Courts of Law, or in the Heads of Departments.

The President shall have Power to fill up all Vacancies that may happen during the Recess of the Senate, by granting Commissions which shall expire at the End of their next Session.

Section 3. He shall from time to time give to the Congress Information of the State of the Union, and recommend to their Consideration such Measures as he shall judge necessary and expedient; he may, on extraordinary Occasions, convene both Houses, or either of them, and in Case of Disagreement between them, with Respect to the Time of Adjournment, he may adjourn them to such Time as he shall think proper; he shall receive Ambassadors and other public Ministers; he shall take Care that the Laws be faithfully executed, and shall Commission all the Officers of the United States.

Section 4. The President, Vice President and all civil Officers of the United States, shall be removed from Office on Impeachment for, and Conviction of, Treason, Bribery, or other high Crimes and Misdemeanors.

Article III

Section 1. The judicial Power of the United States, shall be vested in one supreme Court, and in such inferior Courts as the Congress may from time to time ordain and establish. The Judges, both of the supreme and inferior Courts, shall hold their Offices during good Behaviour, and shall, at stated Times, receive for their Services, a Compensation, which shall not be diminished during their Continuance in Office.

Section 2. The judicial Power shall extend to all Cases, in Law and Equity, arising under this Constitution, the Laws of the United States, and Treaties made, or which shall be made, under their Authority;—to all Cases affecting Ambassadors, other public Ministers and Consuls;—to all Cases of admiralty and maritime Jurisdiction;—to Controversies to which the United States shall be a Party;—to Controversies between two or more States;—[*between a State and Citizens of another State;—*][8] between Citizens of different States;—between Citizens of the same State claiming Lands under Grants of different States, [*and between a State, or the Citizens thereof, and foreign States, Citizens or Subjects.*][9]

In all Cases affecting Ambassadors, other public Ministers and Consuls, and those in which a State shall be Party, the supreme Court shall have original Jurisdiction. In all the other Cases before mentioned, the supreme Court shall have appellate Jurisdiction, both as to Law and Fact, with such Exceptions, and under such Regulations as the Congress shall make.

The Trial of all Crimes, except in Cases of Impeachment, shall be by Jury; and such Trial shall be held in the State where the said Crimes shall have been committed; but when not committed within any State, the Trial shall be at such Place or Places as the Congress may by Law have directed.

Section 3. Treason against the United States, shall consist only in levying War against them, or in adhering to their Enemies, giving them Aid and Comfort. No Person shall be convicted of Treason unless on the Testimony of two Witnesses to the same overt Act, or on Confession in open Court.

The Congress shall have Power to declare the Punishment of Treason, but no Attainder of Treason shall work Corruption of Blood, or Forfeiture except during the Life of the Person attained.

Article IV

Section 1. Full Faith and Credit shall be given in each State to the public Acts, Records, and judicial Proceedings of every other State. And the Congress may by general Laws prescribe the Manner in which such Acts, Records and Proceedings shall be proved, and the Effect thereof.

Section 2. The Citizens of each State shall be entitled to all Privileges and Immunities of Citizens in the several States.

A Person charged in any State with Treason, Felony, or other Crime, who shall flee from Justice, and be found in another State, shall on Demand of

---

[8] superseded by the Eleventh Amendment
[9] superseded by the Eleventh Amendment

the executive Authority of the State from which he fled, be delivered up, to be removed to the State having Jurisdiction of the Crime.

[No Person held to Service or Labour in one State, under the Laws thereof, escaping into another, shall, in Consequence of any Law or Regulation therein, be discharged from such Service or Labour, but shall be delivered up on Claim of the Party to whom such Service or Labour may be due.][10]

Section 3. New States may be admitted by the Congress into this Union; but no new State shall be formed or erected within the Jurisdiction of any other State; nor any State be formed by the Junction of two or more States, or Parts of States, without the Consent of the Legislatures of the States concerned as well as of the Congress.

The Congress shall have Power to dispose of and make all needful Rules and Regulations respecting the Territory or other Property belonging to the United States; and nothing in this Constitution shall be so construed as to Prejudice any Claims of the United States, or of any particular State.

Section 4. The United States shall guarantee to every State in this Union a Republican Form of Government, and shall protect each of them against Invasion; and on Application of the Legislature, or of the Executive (when the Legislature cannot be convened) against domestic Violence.

Article V

The Congress, whenever two thirds of both Houses shall deem it necessary, shall propose Amendments to this Constitution, or, on the Application of the Legislatures of two thirds of the several States, shall call a Convention for proposing Amendments, which, in either Case, shall be valid to all Intents and Purposes, as Part of this Constitution, when ratified by the Legislatures of three fourths of the several States, or by Conventions in three fourths thereof, as the one or the other Mode of Ratification may be proposed by the Congress; Provided that no Amendment which may be made prior to the Year One thousand eight hundred and eight shall in any Manner affect the first and fourth Clauses in the Ninth Section of the first Article; and that no State, without its Consent, shall be deprived of its equal Suffrage in the Senate.

---

[10] superseded by the Thirteenth Amendment

Article VI

All Debts contracted and Engagements entered into, before the Adoption of this Constitution, shall be as valid against the United States under this Constitution, as under the Confederation.

This Constitution, and the Laws of the United States which shall be made in Pursuance thereof; and all Treaties made, or which shall be made, under the Authority of the United States, shall be the supreme Law of the Land; and the Judges in every State shall be bound thereby, any Thing in the Constitution or Laws of any State to the Contrary notwithstanding.

The Senators and Representatives before mentioned, and the Members of the several State Legislatures, and all executive and judicial Officers, both of the United States and of the several States, shall be bound by Oath or Affirmation, to support this Constitution; but no religious Test shall ever be required as a Qualification to any Office or public Trust under the United States.

Article VII

The Ratification of the Conventions of nine States, shall be sufficient for the Establishment of this Constitution between the States so ratifying the Same.

Done in Convention by the Unanimous Consent of the States present the Seventeenth Day of September in the Year of our Lord one thousand seven hundred and Eighty seven and of the Independence of the United States of America the Twelfth In Witness whereof We have hereunto subscribed our Names,

Go. Washington—
Presidt. and deputy from Virginia

New Hampshire
John Langdon
Nicholas Gilman

Massachusetts
Nathaniel Gorham
Rufus King

Connecticut
Wm. Saml. Johnson
Roger Sherman

New York
Alexander Hamilton

New Jersey
Wil: Livingston
David Brearley
Wm. Paterson
Jona: Dayton

Pennsylvania
B Franklin

Thomas Mifflin
Robt. Morris
Geo. Clymer
Thos. FitzSimons
Jared Ingersoll
James Wilson
Gouv Morris

Delaware
Geo: Read
Gunning Bedford jun
John Dickinson
Richard Bassett
Jaco: Broom

Maryland
James McHenry
Dan of St Thos. Jenifer
Danl. Carroll

Virginia
John Blair—
James Madison Jr.

North Carolina
Wm. Blount
Richd. Dobbs Spaight
Hu Williamson

South Carolina
J. Rutledge
Charles Cotesworth Pinckney
Charles Pinckney
Pierce Butler

Georgia
William Few
Abr Baldwin

Attest William Jackson Secretary

AMENDMENTS TO THE CONSTITUTION OF THE UNITED STATES OF AMERICA

Amendment I

Ratified December 15, 1791

Congress shall make no law respecting an establishment of religion, or prohibiting the free exercise thereof; or abridging the freedom of speech, or of the press; or the right of the people peaceably to assemble, and to petition the Government for a redress of grievances.

Amendment II

Ratified December 15, 1791

A well regulated Militia, being necessary to the security of a free State, the right of the people to keep and bear Arms, shall not be infringed.

Amendment III

Ratified December 15, 1791

No Soldier shall, in time of peace be quartered in any house, without the consent of the Owner, nor in time of war, but in a manner to be prescribed by law.

Amendment IV

Ratified December 15, 1791

The right of the people to be secure in their persons, houses, papers, and effects, against unreasonable searches and seizures, shall not be violated, and no Warrants shall issue, but upon probable cause, supported by Oath or affirmation, and particularly describing the place to be searched, and the persons or things to be seized.

Amendment V

Ratified December 15, 1791

No person shall be held to answer for a capital, or otherwise infamous crime, unless on a presentment or indictment of a Grand Jury, except in cases arising in the land or naval forces, or in the Militia, when in actual service in time of War or public danger; nor shall any person be subject for the same offence to be twice put in jeopardy of life or limb, nor shall be compelled in any criminal case to be a witness against himself, nor be deprived of life, liberty, or property, without due process of law; nor shall private property be taken for public use, without just compensation.

Amendment VI

Ratified December 15, 1791

In all criminal prosecutions, the accused shall enjoy the right to a speedy and public trial, by an impartial jury of the State and district wherein the crime shall have been committed, which district shall have been previously ascertained by law, and to be informed of the nature and cause of the accusation; to be confronted with the witnesses against him; to have compulsory process for obtaining witnesses in his favor, and to have the assistance of counsel for his defence.

Amendment VII

Ratified December 15, 1791

In Suits at common law, where the value in controversy shall exceed twenty dollars, the right of trial by jury shall be preserved, and no fact tried by a jury, shall be otherwise reexamined in any Court of the United States, than according to the rules of the common law.

Amendment VIII

Ratified December 15, 1791

Excessive bail shall not be required, nor excessive fines imposed, nor cruel and unusual punishments inflicted.

Amendment IX

Ratified December 15, 1791

The enumeration in the Constitution, of certain rights, shall not be construed to deny or disparage others retained by the people.

Amendment X

Ratified December 15, 1791

The powers not delegated to the United States by the Constitution, nor prohibited by it to the States, are reserved to the States respectively, or to the people.

APPENDIX E

Suggestions For Further Reading

Banning, Lance. *Jefferson and Madison*. Madison, WI: Madison House, 1995.

Blackstone, William. *Commentaries on the Laws of England*. Oxford: Clarendon Press, 1765.

Bloom, Sol. *History of the Formation of the Union Under the Constitution*. Washington DC: Government Printing Office, 1943.

Cogan, Neil H., editor. *The Complete Bill of Rights: The Drafts, Debates, Sources, and Origins*. Oxford: Oxford University Press, 1997.

Commager, Henry Steele, editor. *Documents of American History*. New York: Appleton-Century-Crofts, 1968.

Conley, Patrick T, and John P. Kaminski, editors. *The Bill of Rights and the States: The Colonial and Revolutionary origins of American Liberties*. Madison, WI: Madison House, 1992.

Davis, G. R. C. *Magna Carta*. London: The Trustees of the British Museum, 1963.

Deane, Charles, editor. *History of Plymouth Plantation by William Bradford*. Boston: Privately Printed, 1856.

Ferling, John. *A Leap in the Dark: The Struggle to Create the American Republic*. Oxford: Oxford University Press, 2003.

Gales, Joseph, Sr., editor. *Annals of Congress*. Washington, DC: Government Printing Office, 1834.

Handlin, Oscar, and Mary Handlin, editors. *The Popular Sources of Political Authority: Documents on the Massachusetts Constitution of 1780*. Cambridge, MA: Belknap Press of Harvard University Press, 1966.

Hening, W. W. *Statutes at Large*. Richmond: George Cochran, 1823.

Hunt, Gaillard, editor. *The Writings of James Madison*. New York: G.P. Putman's Sons, 1900–1910.

Hutchinson, et. al., editors. *The Papers of James Madison*. 19 volumes. Chicago: University of Chicago Press, 1967.

Jennings, Sir Ivan. *Magna Carta and Its Influence in the World Today*. London: Her Majesty's Stationery, 1965.

Katz, Stanley N., editor. *Commentaries on the Laws of England*. Chicago: University of Chicago Press, 1979.

Kukla, Jon, editor. *The Bill of Rights: A Lively Heritage*. Richmond: Virginia State Library and Archives, 1987.

Kurland, Philip B., and Ralph Lerner, editors. *The Founders' Constitution*. Five Volumes. Chicago: University of Chicago Press, 1987.

Labunski, Richard. *James Madison and the Struggle for the Bill of Rights*. Oxford: Oxford University Press, 2006.

Lloyd, Gordon, and Margie Lloyd, editors. *The Essential Bill of Rights*. Lanham, Maryland: University Press of America, 1998.

Maier, Pauline. *American Scripture: Making of the Declaration of Independence*. New York: Vintage, 1997.

Riemer, Neal. *James Madison: Creating the American Constitution*. Washington, DC: Congressional Quarterly Inc, 1986.

Rutland, Robert Allen, et. al., editors. *The Papers of James Madison*. Chicago: University of Chicago Press. 1975.

Rutland, Robert Allen. *The Birth of the Bill of Rights, 1776–1791*. Boston: Northeastern University Press, 1983.

Schechter, Stephen L., and Richard Bernstein, editors. *The Contexts of the Bill of Rights*. Albany, New York: New York State Commission on the Bicentennial of the Constitution, 1990.

Schwartz, Bernard, editor. *The Roots of the Bill of Rights*. Five Volumes. New York: Chelsea House Publishers, 1980.

Schwartz, Bernard. *The Great Rights of Mankind: A History of the American Bill of Rights*. Madison, WI: Madison House, 1992.

Swindler, William F., editor. *Sources and Documents of United States Constitutions*. Dobbs Ferry, NY: Oceana Publications, 1973.

Tansill, Charles. *Documents Illustrative of the Formation of the Union of the United States*. Washington, DC: Government Printing Office, 1927.

Thorpe, F.N., editor. *The Federal and State Constitutions*. Seven Volumes. Washington, DC: Government Printing Office, 1909.

Veit, Helen, Kenneth Bowling, and Charles Bangs Bickford, editors. *Creating the Bill of Rights: The Documentary Record of the First Federal Congress*. Baltimore: Johns Hopkins University Press, 1991.

Wood, Gordon S. *The Creation of the American Republic, 1776–1787*. New York: W. W. Norton & Sons, 1969.